# The Trouble with Sharing

*Interpersonal Challenges in Peer-to-Peer Exchange*

# Synthesis Lectures on Human-Centered Informatics

Editor
**John M. Carroll**, *Penn State University*

Human-Centered Informatics (HCI) is the intersection of the cultural, the social, the cognitive, and the aesthetic with computing and information technology. It encompasses a huge range of issues, theories, technologies, designs, tools, environments, and human experiences in knowledge work, recreation and leisure activity, teaching and learning, and the potpourri of everyday life. The series publishes state-of-the-art syntheses, case studies, and tutorials in key areas. It shares the focus of leading international conferences in HCI.

The Trouble with Sharing: Interpersonal Challenges in Peer-to-Peer Exchange
Airi Lampinen

Interface for an App—The Design Rationale Leading to an App that Allows Someone with Type 1 Diabetes to Self-Manage their Condition
Bob Spence

Organizational Implementation: The Design in Use of Information Systems
Morten Hertzum

Data-Driven Personas
Bernard J. Jansen, Joni Salminen, Soon-gyo Jung, Kathleen Guan

Worth-Focused Design, Book 2: Approaches, Context, and Case Studies
Gilbert Cockton

Worth-Focused Design, Book 1: Balance, Integration, and Generosity
Gilbert Cockton

Statistics for HCI: Making Sense of Quantitative Data
Alan Dix

Usability Testing
Morten Hertzum

*For Nuuti and all the kids in his generation*

The Trouble with Sharing: Interpersonal Challenges in Peer-to-Peer
Exchange Airi Lampinen

ISBN: 978-3-031-01106-1     print
ISBN: 978-3-031-02234-0     ebook
ISBN: 978-3-031-00214-4     hardcover

DOI 10.1007/978-3-031-02234-0

A Publication in the Springer series
*SYNTHESIS LECTURES ON HUMAN-CENTERED INFORMATICS*
Lecture #51
Series Editor: John M. Carroll, Penn State University

Series ISSN  1946-7680  Print  1946-7699  Electronic

# The Trouble with Sharing

*Interpersonal Challenges in Peer-to-Peer Exchange*

Airi Lampinen
Stockholm University

*SYNTHESIS LECTURES ON HUMAN-CENTERED INFORMATICS #51*

# ABSTRACT

Peer-to-peer exchange is a type of sharing that involves the transfer of valued resources, such as goods and services, among members of a local community and/or between parties who have not met before the exchange encounter. It involves online systems that allow strangers to exchange in ways that were previously confined to the realm of kinship and friendship. Through the examples in this book, we encounter attempts to foster the sharing of goods and services in local communities and consider the intricacies of sharing homes temporarily with strangers (also referred to as hospitality exchange or network hospitality). Some of the exchange arrangements discussed involve money while others explicitly ban participants from using it. All rely on digital technologies, but the trickiest challenges have more to do with social interaction than technical features. This book explores what makes peer-to-peer exchange challenging, with an emphasis on reciprocity, closeness, and participation: How should we reciprocate? How might we manage interactions with those we encounter to attain some closeness but not too much? What keeps people from getting involved or draws them into exchange activities that they would rather avoid?

This book adds to the growing body of research on exchange platforms and the sharing economy. It provides empirical examples and conceptual grounding for thinking about interpersonal challenges in peer-to-peer exchange and the efforts that are required for exchange arrangements to flourish. It offers inspiration for how we might think and design differently to better understand and support the efforts of those involved in peer-to-peer exchange. While the issues cannot be simply "solved" by technology, it matters which digital tools an exchange arrangement relies on, and even seemingly small design decisions can have a significant impact on what it is like to participate in exchange processes. The technologies that support exchange arrangements—often platforms of some sort—can be driven by differing sets of values and commitments. This book invites students and scholars in the Human–Computer Interaction community, and beyond, to envision and design alternative exchange arrangements and future economies.

## KEYWORDS

sharing economy, exchange platforms, peer-to-peer exchange, network hospitality, social exchange

# Contents

# Preface

Shortly after industry experts Rachel Botsman and Roo Rogers published their 2010 book *What's Mine Is Yours: The Rise of Collaborative Consumption* (which went on to become something of a bible for sharing enthusiasts), Botsman's book tour made a stop in San Francisco. I lived in Berkeley at the time and while the topic had little to do with my research focus back then, I was full of curiosity about peer-to-peer exchange and the rising hype about the sharing economy. So, on a late summer evening, I ventured to the city and took a seat in a room full of other curious people. This was when I first heard the narratives that have since become so familiar and so contested: In the aftermath of the financial crisis of 2008, here was a vision of something that could help us economically, socially, and environmentally, all at once. With the help of digital technologies, ordinary people would come together to cooperate, help one another, and co-use their existing resources. Too good to be true? With the wisdom of hindsight, it is now all too easy to apply a critical lens on the talks that were given that evening. I do not want to downplay the excitement I felt in the moment, though, as I was listening eagerly, scribbling down notes, and experiencing the magic of having stumbled into the right room at the right time.

In less than a decade, the narrative of the sharing economy shifted from early enthusiasm and widely-hyped promise to a story many consider best told in the past tense. Journalist Susie Cagle's 2019 piece[1] "*The sharing economy was always a scam*" describes how "sharing" was supposed to save us but how it, instead, became a Trojan horse for a precarious economic future. Cagle argues that the so-called sharing economy "*promised to activate underutilized assets in order to sustain a healthier world and build community trust*" and that it was supposed to "*let strangers around the world maximize the utility of every possession to the benefit of all.*" Her verdict is stern: "*Sharing was supposed to transform our world for the better. Instead, the only thing we're sharing is the mess it left behind.*" Cagle is not alone in voicing her critique. Neal Gorenflo, a longstanding vocal proponent of sharing, agrees that the story so far is highly unsatisfactory: "*You may have heard enough about the sharing economy for a lifetime during the peak of its hype a few years ago—but that was just the beginning of its development as an economic paradigm. It was an awkward first step given the astounding number of broken laws, fines, and false promises its headliners, Airbnb and Uber, left in their wake.*"[2]

Yet, Gorenflo's overall conclusion is optimistic: "*The sharing economy has only just begun.*" It is both easy and tempting to agree with Gorenflo's reasoning: "*In fact, we need sharing more now than ever as climate change, unprecedented wealth inequality and social division shake the very foundations of*

---

[1] https://onezero.medium.com/the-sharing-economy-was-always-a-scam-68a9b36f3e4b (read on June 4, 2021).
[2] https://www.nesta.org.uk/feature/sharing-economy-has-only-just-begun/ (read on June 4, 2021).

*our civilization. Moreover, it's unlikely these challenges can be addressed individually—we need systemic solutions to a systemic challenge."* There are troubled times ahead, and I continue to believe that peer-to-peer exchange holds potential as one path to collective responses to the social, economic, and environmental crises we are facing. This book is in part an invitation to return to where the story of the sharing economy began: peer-to-peer arrangements intended to facilitate the co-use of resources and to encourage reciprocal acts of kindness and sociability.

Neighborly help and strangers extending hospitality to one another can sound quaint. Peer-to-peer exchange, especially when money is not changing hands, can be framed as leisurely or intriguing—something new and appealing but hardly consequential enough to leave much of a mark on everyday life. Yet, such exchange arrangements can provide resources and support that are desperately needed. Historically, those who most need support from their local community and who have the least access to mainstream market solutions are the likeliest to be actively involved in peer-to-peer activities (Nembhard, 2014). When buying goods and services from the primary market is difficult for one reason or another—be it a lack of economic means, prohibitive distances, or discriminatory practices—people band together to survive, creating local alternatives. But as the name of the book suggests, there is trouble with sharing: Peer-to-peer exchange is an idea that is easy to love in the abstract but that can be difficult to carry out in practice.

On a systemic level, with the cascading crises of the 21st century, it is worth asking how our outlook on peer-to-peer exchange would change if we approached it less as an option and more as a necessary start on rethinking how we live together on this planet. This book, then, is also a plea to keep at the work we have started, despite the problems and challenges the sharing economy entails. Even as the early hype has fizzled out, there remain important research topics and design challenges that scholars in the Human–Computer Interaction community—and beyond—are well positioned to take on.

# Acknowledgments

This book brings together various strands of research into peer-to-peer exchange: The empirical accounts draw on a collection of studies conducted together with a number of colleagues over many years. The key analytic ideas that I develop in this book are also rooted in collaborative research efforts. As such, I want to make clear that while this is a single-authored book, in many ways, this book is as much as my collaborators' as it is mine. In particular, I wish to highlight my co-authors on the empirical work: Emmi Maijanen (née Suhonen), Tapio Ikkala, Vilma Lehtinen, Coye Cheshire, Kai Huotari, and Judd Antin. Since the very beginning of my interest in the sharing economy, Juho Makkonen and Antti Virolainen—the co-founders of Sharetribe—have been important sounding boards and inspirational thinkers in their own right. During the writing of this book, Barry Brown, Rob Comber, Moira McGregor, Chiara Rossitto, Ann Light, Coye Cheshire, and Mary L. Gray have been invaluable colleagues to think with. Conversations and collaborations with them have shaped this text in crucial ways. However, all responsibility for the errors and shortcomings is mine.

I would also like to thank everyone who has supported me with the writing of this book, including our entire Stockholm Technology and Interaction Research (STIR) group, members of the From Sharing to Caring COST Action, and the Social Media Collective at Microsoft Research New England. Barry Brown, Minna Saariketo, Riyaz Sheikh, and Ville Sundberg provided helpful feedback on the manuscript. Riyaz Sheikh also created the cover art for the book, bringing its spirit to life in visual form.

I thank Diane D. Cerra from Morgan and Claypool Publishers and Series Editor John M. Carroll for their patient support and advice, along with arranging a wonderful set of feedback from expert readers. I am grateful for the reviews: they guided me to improve the manuscript.

Finally, I thank my parents and siblings for their support and for teaching me how to share. My husband Ville Sundberg has given his unwavering support and encouragement for this project from start to finish, while ensuring that I never forget that I am not my work. This book is dedicated to our son Nuuti.

The text draws on material from the following published journal and conference articles:
Suhonen, E., Lampinen, A., Cheshire, C., and Antin, J. (2010, November). Everyday favors: a case study of a local online gift exchange system. In *Proceedings of the 16th ACM International Conference on Supporting Group Work* (pp. 11-20). DOI: 10.1145/1880071.1880074.

Lampinen, A., Lehtinen, V., Cheshire, C., and Suhonen, E. (2013, February). Indebtedness and reciprocity in local online exchange. In *Proceedings of the 2013 Conference on Computer Supported Cooperative Work* (pp. 661-672). DOI: 10.1145/2441776.2441850.

Ikkala, T. and Lampinen, A. (2014, February). Defining the price of hospitality: networked hospitality exchange via Airbnb. In *Proceedings of the Companion Publication of the 17th Acm Conference on Computer Supported Cooperative Work and Social Computing* (pp. 173-176). DOI: 10.1145/2556420.2556506.

Lampinen, A. (2014, February). Account sharing in the context of networked hospitality exchange. In *Proceedings of the 17th ACM Conference on Computer Supported Cooperative Work and Social Computing* (pp. 499-504). DOI: 10.1145/2531602.2531665.

Lampinen, A., Huotari, K. J. E., and Cheshire, C. (2015). Challenges to participation in the sharing economy: the case of local online peer-to-peer exchange in a single parents' network. *Interaction Design and Architecture(s)*. Available at http://www.mifav.uniroma2.it/inevent/events/idea2010/doc/24_1.pdf.

Ikkala, T. and Lampinen, A. (2015, February). Monetizing network hospitality: Hospitality and sociability in the context of Airbnb. In *Proceedings of the 18th ACM Conference on Computer Supported Cooperative Work and Social Computing* (pp. 1033-1044). DOI: 10.1145/2675133.2675274.

Lampinen, A. and Cheshire, C. (2016, May). Hosting via Airbnb: Motivations and financial assurances in monetized network hospitality. In *Proceedings of the 2016 CHI Conference on Human Factors in Computing Systems* (pp. 1669-1680). DOI: 10.1145/2858036.2858092.

Lampinen, A. (2016). Hosting together via Couchsurfing: Privacy management in the context of network hospitality. *International Journal of Communication*, 10, 20 (pp. 1581-1600).

Lampinen, A. and Brown, B. (2017, May). Market design for HCI: Successes and failures of peer-to-peer exchange platforms. In *Proceedings of the 2017 CHI Conference on Human Factors in Computing Systems* (pp. 4331-4343). DOI: 10.1145/3025453.3025515.

Lampinen, A., McGregor, M., Comber, R., and Brown, B. (2018). Member-owned alternatives: exploring participatory forms of organising with cooperatives. *Proceedings of the ACM on Human-Computer Interaction*, 2(CSCW), 1-19. DOI: 10.1145/3274369.

# CHAPTER 1

# Introduction

Think of going on a holiday. Bringing along only what you need during your trip, you leave most of what you own at home. Why not let a friend use your bike? And maybe you could rent out some of the camping gear you rarely get around to using? You might ask a neighbor to water the flowers for you—or you might opt to make some money by letting a guest enjoy the comforts of your home.

But what if the friend breaks the bike, the camping gear goes missing, and the neighbor loses your keys? Beyond such evident problems, you might worry about the hassles of coordinating all of this. The dance of asking and offering, and then thanking and not-even-mentioning-it, may feel awkward. Will receiving help from the neighbor leave you in a debt of gratitude? What if the house guest is nosey and pokes around in your wardrobe? Might your neighbors be bothered by a stranger staying at your place?

Therein lies the trouble with sharing.

This book focuses on *peer-to-peer exchange*, a type of sharing that involves the transfer of valued resources, such as goods and services, among members of a local community and/or between parties who have not met before the exchange encounter. It involves online systems that allow strangers to exchange in ways that were previously confined to the realm of kinship and friendship. This book considers the interpersonal challenges in this type of exchange activity: How should we reciprocate? How might we manage interactions with those we encounter so as to attain some closeness—but not too much? What keeps people from getting involved or draws them into exchange activities that they would rather avoid? This book describes how people seek to address questions such as these as they engage in peer-to-peer exchange. It also considers how purposeful design might help them in doing so.

This book focuses on two types of peer-to-peer exchange: First, we encounter attempts to foster the sharing of goods and services in local communities. This type of sharing can include lending and borrowing camping gear, giving away furniture one no longer wants, or helping a neighbor fix their bike. Second, we will consider the intricacies of sharing homes temporarily with strangers (also referred to as hospitality exchange or network hospitality). In this domain, we focus on Airbnb and Couchsurfing, two online systems that disrupt the traditional corporate business models associated with rental housing and hospitality: Instead of a single company managing buildings, terms, and leases, these platforms facilitate connections between hosts and guests. Airbnb facilitates short-term rentals with a clearly defined price, while Couchsurfing explicitly prohibits guests from making monetary payments to hosts, relying instead on the expectation that guests will "pay it forward" by providing hospitality to somebody else in the future.

The examples that I draw upon all rely on digital technologies, but as will become obvious, the trickiest challenges with peer-to-peer exchange have more to do with social interaction than technical features. The issues those involved in peer-to-peer exchange face cannot be simply "solved" by technology. Yet, it matters which digital tools an exchange arrangement relies on, and even seemingly small design decisions can have a significant impact on what it is like to participate in exchange processes. The technologies that support exchange arrangements—often platforms of some sort—can be driven by differing sets of values and commitments. There is room to envision and design alternative exchange arrangements and future economies.

When observed on the ground, interpersonal dynamics in peer-to-peer exchange do not always play out in ways that match designers' and community activists' ideals and aspirations. Considering this helps us understand why so many exchange arrangements fail. The point of highlighting these challenges is not that we cannot have nice things—the joys and benefits of sharing—but that we must work for them. This book invites us to consider how we might facilitate the efforts that are required for peer-to-peer exchange to flourish.

## 1.1    THE SHARING ECONOMY

This book focuses on two particular subdomains of what has come to be known as the sharing economy. But what is the sharing economy? In addition to pausing briefly to consider efforts at defining the phenomenon, let us begin to answer that question by considering what kinds of exchange activities, online technologies, and discourses the phenomenon encompasses.

### 1.1.1    DEFINITIONS AT THE CROSSROADS OF IDEALS AND REALITIES

Acqueir et al. (2017) locate "*the sharing economy ideal*" at the intersection of three overlapping, yet distinct, phenomena: the access economy, the platform economy, and community-based economy (see Figure 1.1). First, *access economy* refers to arrangements that are focused on sharing underutilized assets to optimize their use. Second, the *platform economy* has to do with intermediating decentralized exchanges (among peers) through a digital platform. Here, the focus is on the platform as an intermediary that creates and facilitates a *multi-sided market*. Simply put, this means that the platform brings together many "buyers" and many "sellers" who exchange directly with one another. For instance, a platform can help those who have something to offer (such as an Airbnb host who wants to get the word out about the space they are renting) to come into contact with those interested in what they have to offer (such as a guest looking for accommodation). Third, *community-based economy* concerns efforts at coordinating through non-contractual, non-hierarchical, or non-monetized forms of interaction. Examples of this can range from Wikipedia to timebanks and neighborly tool sharing schemes. According to Acquier et al. (2017), then, the sharing economy combines these three elements: It is about granting individuals access to underutilized resources in order to optimize usage, with the help of digital platforms that provide exchange opportunities between peers. This framework suggests that the exchanges tend to be non-monetized, non-contractual, and/or non-hierarchical, oriented toward community interactions rather than maximizing profits. While the examples in this book will illustrate that peer-to-peer exchange activities do not necessarily fit neatly with this definition, the framework is helpful in articulating what the sharing economy is supposed to be about—ideally.

Figure 1.1: The Sharing Economy Ideal. Adapted from Acquier et al. (2017).

Belk (2010, 2014) has advanced another influential line of thinking, focusing on sharing—an activity he defines as a consumer behavior that is distinct from both commodity exchange and gift giving. This conceptual mapping can be helpful in understanding why it can be so controversial to apply the term sharing to describe situations that involve monetary exchange. In Belk's definition, sharing is non-ownership-based and nonreciprocal—and if we follow his argument, then monetary exchange or even expectations of reciprocity are not really sharing. However, in popular usage, the term sharing economy now typically refers to a mixture of all of these.

Aligning her conceptualization with how the sharing economy phenomenon has been unfolding in practice, Schor (2016) distinguishes between two main approaches that differ in their market orientation: First, profit-driven digital platforms, such as Airbnb, the taxi service Uber, and TaskRabbit, a marketplace for gig work, generate economic activity by matching providers and consumers to optimize resource use to capacity or by brokering on-demand labor. Second, there is a non-profit approach to the sharing economy that prioritizes social, cultural, and environmental values. Here, we can think of sharing communities like PumpiPumpe that are oriented toward facilitating the co-use of household items and other physical possessions primarily among those who reside near one another (Fedosov et al., 2021). Another common example are timebanks that reward each hour of community volunteering with one credit of a time-based local currency, regardless of the service provided since equality is a key principle (Bellotti et al., 2013; Seyfang, 2003). Both approaches are rooted in long trajectories of organizing economic activity, consumption, and community life. To help us make sense of the sharing economy, Chapter 2 will further situate the phenomenon in its historical and contemporary context, considering it as a part of domains like social exchange, hospitality, marketplaces, and community informatics.

## 1.1.2    DIVERSE DIGITAL TECHNOLOGIES

Peer-to-peer exchange commonly combines online and offline interactions, but digital technology is not always central to it. Sometimes it plays no role at all. Most characterizations of the sharing economy refer to *exchange platforms*. Simply put, these are online forums that support the peer-to-peer exchange of valued resources such as goods and services. What is new and innovative about platforms as online spaces is how they bring about a market form where strangers can (at least sometimes) conduct exchange in ways that were previously confined to the realm of kinship and friendship (Schor and Fitzmaurice, 2015), such as homestays. However, platforms do much more than just mediate peer-to-peer exchange—they spell out and propose through their affordances, more or less forcefully, particular sets of relations among different actors (Ilten, 2015). Platform companies, then, play a crucial role in shaping and regulating the kinds of interactions and exchanges that can take place.

However, all peer-to-peer exchange arrangements do not have networked platforms organizing and driving them. Some rely on commonly available tools, such as Facebook, WhatsApp, and Google Docs, rather than bespoke platforms (Bødker et al., 2016, 2017; Bødker and Klokmose, 2012). Other arrangements may have little to do with digital technologies– just think of windowsills in apartment blocks where neighbors leave old books and used items for others to take, or physical hubs like tiny libraries that serve a similar role on the level of a neighborhood. While the empirical examples in this book feature exchange platforms, I use the term *exchange arrangements* in an expansive way to capture diverse relations to technology.

At the heart of exchange platforms and constellations of digital tools is human–computer interaction (HCI)—how these systems are designed and interacted with is fundamental to the functioning of the social and economic arrangements they bring about. Even small design details can make a big difference in shaping participants' exchange experiences (convenient vs effortful), the style of interpersonal interactions that take place (transactional vs intimate), and the type of trust that enables exchange activities (trusting a platform vs trusting another person). Were it not for this strong link to digital technologies, it might well be that the sharing economy would not have attracted such strong interest from HCI scholars. When we design for new exchange arrangements, we inherently adopt some assumptions about a social system—or create a new one. Markets are made and sustained by those parties involved in their functioning (Lampinen and Brown, 2017). A departure from considering markets as natural mechanisms is crucial for the ideas this book advances, since casting markets as human artifacts turns them into objects of design and critical scrutiny, and as such, more explicitly objects of study for HCI scholars. Since markets are often instantiated in a technological form, the HCI community can take an active role in designing markets and intervening critically where they do not work fairly or effectively.

### 1.1.3   DISCREPANT DISCOURSES

The sharing economy is a phenomenon that entails not only different types of exchange activities and technologies to support them, but also and importantly, discourses. These ways of speaking about sharing (John, 2017) are part of what makes the whole notion of the sharing economy so difficult to define and so easy to contest. For instance, many platforms that have been labelled as part of the sharing economy are mainly about monetizing (underutilized) resources, such as possessions or skills. The sharing economy's promise to combine exchange transactions of the market with the social interaction capacities of communities prompts ambiguities and tensions (Acquier et al., 2017). The apparent contradiction of fostering genuine community connections while maintaining room for commercial activity and monetized exchange has been at the heart of a lot of the debate regarding platforms and sharing (Barta and Neff, 2016; Lampinen, 2015). While economic and social exchange often intertwine, the relationship between commercial values and community values can be fraught (Barta and Neff, 2016).

Given the lack of an agreed-upon definition, the term sharing economy gets used to refer to such a diversity of activities and arrangements that the competing and conflicting meanings risk rendering it meaningless. The term has been, for good reasons, heavily critiqued in academic writing, often in a move to propose another term, presumably with the hope that another word could both rid the concept of its baggage and better capture what the respective authors have considered essential and worth studying. In this book, I purposefully avoid engaging with controversies over what should be seen as rightfully part of the *real* sharing economy in contrast to what is fake or insincere and, as such, needs to be called out for masquerading as sharing. Instead, I draw inspiration from María Puig de la Bellacasa's (2017) writing on the notion of care and the call to reclaim it, in part by "*acknowledging the poisons in our grounds rather than searching for a pure alternative or definitive critique.*" There is too much that is important in the phenomenon that has come to be known and critiqued as the sharing economy for us to give up on it entirely.

While the term does little as an analytical concept, it has emerged as an effective call of summons to bring together scholars and practitioners who care for and work on an interconnected set of issues, loosely having to do with how spaces, goods, capital, and labor are exchanged between individuals, typically with the help of networked technologies (which are most often referred to as platforms). Second, even if we wanted to apply more meaningful terminology, it would be hard to do away with the *sharing economy* wholly given how stubbornly the term persists in both popular and academic usage. Proposing another path forward, Chapter 3 offers scoping questions that are meant to help in distinguishing different parts of the sharing economy phenomenon and articulating particular points of emphasis in an analytically productive way.

## 1.2    INTERPERSONAL CHALLENGES IN PEER-TO-PEER EXCHANGE

This book focuses on interpersonal challenges in peer-to-peer exchange with an emphasis on three key themes: reciprocity, closeness, and participation. The chapters corresponding to each theme provide conceptual grounding for thinking about the challenges and offer inspiration for how we might think and design differently to better understand and support participants' efforts. The empirical examples—hospitality exchange and peer-to-peer exchange of goods and services—all involve a digital platform of some sort. Yet, the trickiest challenges with peer-to-peer exchange have more to do with social interaction than technical features. Let us now consider each of the three challenges in turn.

### 1.2.1    RECIPROCITY AND INDEBTEDNESS

The social dynamics of asking for, giving, and receiving help are fraught. Reciprocity and indebtedness—the challenge covered in Chapter 4—are two closely related issues that should be crucial concerns for any socio-technical system designed to facilitate and encourage social exchange. The desire to be—or at least appear—self-sufficient can be strong, and beyond the expected awkwardness of asking for help, an aversion to indebtedness may lead potential exchange partners to be unwilling to accept gifts or help, especially if they do not expect to be capable of reciprocation in the future. Since reciprocity is a core norm of social interaction, it is also an important issue that needs to be tackled for peer-to-peer exchange arrangements to flourish. However, along with positive benefits of solidarity from acts of reciprocity, there are also psychological and interpersonal challenges to reckon with. Be it a system built around clear-cut transactions, direct barter between exchange partners, or generalized reciprocity on the level of a community, exchange always involves some type of reciprocation. To help us address challenges related to reciprocity and indebtedness, Chapter 4 lays out different forms and layers of reciprocity. It features example cases of peer-to-peer exchange to, first, discuss how fears of indebtedness can be a deterrent to peer-to-peer exchange, in parallel or more so than fears of being taken advantage of by freeloaders, and second, to argue that even when money is an obvious and effective means for balancing out an exchange, it alone is often not enough for peer-to-peer exchange to unfold in a satisfactory—or at least not an enjoyable—manner. Exchange experiences are always shaped by how reciprocation is handled. As such, when we design for peer-to-peer exchange, we can introduce different modes of exchange purposefully to foster desired social qualities.

## 1.2.2   CLOSENESS AND INTIMACY

The second challenge concerns the social dynamics regarding intimacy and closeness in peer-to-peer exchange. These are examined in Chapter 5. After conceptual grounding focused on interpersonal boundary regulation (Altman, 1975; Petronio, 2002), the chapter provides empirical examples that, taken together, frame intimacy and closeness as a key interactional challenge in peer-to-peer exchange in general and network hospitality in particular. Couchsurfing and the early Airbnb both focused on in-person encounters and often intense social interaction among hosts and guests. Meeting locals while traveling and sharing personal stories and communal meals with strangers was key to the narrative. Over the years, Couchsurfing has largely retained this ethos while Airbnb has transformed so that it now, more and more frequently, features clear-cut transactions where hosts and guests meet face-to-face only in the passing or, quite commonly, not at all. Here, I will describe how face-to-face encounters are not always pleasant or desired, but that social interaction that brings about intimacy necessarily requires effort from those involved. I will also make the case that the presence of a monetary transaction at the root of a hospitality exchange—the model familiar to many from Airbnb—does not rule out sociability but can, on the contrary, even facilitate further social exchange. Finally, by turning our focus from face-to-face interaction to the intimacy of homes and possessions, I convey how face-to-face interaction is not the only possible source of a sense of intimacy among exchange partners. The chapter illustrates that interpersonal encounters are necessarily vulnerable and effortful. To foster desired social qualities, then, we may need to nudge those involved to do the work that their preferred outcomes require, regardless of whether the aim is to uphold a sense of distance characteristic of impersonal transacting or to foster a more intimate connection akin to an encounter with a friend. We should also be mindful that these qualities vary by case and that they may not match what those designing a system had in mind. We should be cautious not to assume that closeness should (or could) always be a characteristic of successful peer-to-peer exchange.

## 1.2.3   PARTICIPATION AND INCLUSION

Finally, the book explores how we might better address issues of participation and inclusion—the theme of Chapter 6—when it comes to peer-to-peer exchange. Attracting and fostering participation is an obvious concern for any socio-technical system designed to facilitate peer-to-peer activities—and so should be the closely related notion of inclusion that invites us to reckon with questions of power by attending to what makes it easy for some and difficult for others to take part. Prior research has often addressed issues of trust, motivation, and critical mass to make sense of why some systems succeed in gaining traction while others struggle to foster activity over time (see, e.g., Balestra et al., 2017, 2016; Bellotti et al., 2015; Cheshire, 2011; Kraut and Resnick, 2012; Lampinen and Brown, 2017; Markus, 1987).

While these are fundamental aspects relevant to the dynamics of participation, there is more to the matter than that. Here, I argue for the importance of recognizing the requirements central to participation in different types of exchange. The discussion of participation and inclusion in peer-to-peer exchange draws on examples from both hospitality exchange and local exchange arrangements for goods and services. It addresses discriminatory outcomes, barriers to participation both on the level of individuals and communities, and implications to indirect stakeholders. First, where there is an emphasis on sociability and interpersonal trust, discrimination is connected with homophily—the tendency of people to prefer engaging with others who are similar to them. Second, individuals' motivation is of little help if there are structural barriers blocking their participation, such as scarcity traps or community-level dynamics that make it unlikely for participants to find people well matched to exchange with them. Moreover, alongside unwanted exclusion from peer-to-peer exchange, we also need to account for unwanted inclusion and the implications exchange activities may have on a range of indirect stakeholders (see e.g., Gurran et al., 2020). For example, when it comes to hosting couchsurfers, household members sometimes get drawn into accommodating visitors against their preferences, and stories of neighbors being impacted by the flow of Airbnb guests in their building abound.

## 1.3    RESEARCH SITE AND METHODS

Throughout the book I draw on both primary and secondary sources to explicate interpersonal challenges that make peer-to-peer exchange a demanding undertaking—one fraught with uncertainty but also with the potential of engaging, sometimes intimate, social encounters.

There is no way for one book to handle the whole of the sharing economy, if we want to examine the topic in any detail. Here, I have chosen to focus on two domains: (1) peer-to-peer exchange of goods and services in local communities and (2) hospitality exchange via Couchsurfing and Airbnb. Sideboxes 1.1 and 1.2 tell the story of the research that this book draws upon, for each domain respectively. The empirical backbone of this book is a set of five case studies. Table 1.1 summarizes the cases, the methods that were used, and previous publications on these studies. While each study was originally conducted as a standalone research effort, the earlier ones inevitably informed the later ones. Even more importantly, the studies are linked together by their shared focus on how interpersonal challenges are negotiated in the course of exchange processes.

Table 1.1: Summary of empirical research

| Case | Material and methods | Publication(s) |
| --- | --- | --- |
| Peer-to-peer exchange system Kassi in a Finnish student community | Activity logs, a two-wave survey on usage of the system, and 11 semi-structured individual interviews with community members. Material-driven analytical approach, with framing from the perspective of social exchange theory. | Suhonen, E., Lampinen, A., Cheshire, C., and Antin, J. (2010, November). Lampinen, A., Lehtinen, V., Cheshire, C., and Suhonen, E. (2013, February). |
| Peer-to-peer exchange system Kassi in an American single parents' network | Action research, including an iterative co-design process, participant observation, and 13 semi-structured interviews with network members. Material-driven analytical approach, with framing from the perspective of social exchange theory. | Lampinen, A., Huotari, K. J. E., and Cheshire, C. (2015). |
| Hosting via the hospitality exchange platform Couchsurfing in the US | Semi-structured interviews with 17 people from 9 households who host (or have hosted) guests via Couchsurfing. Material-driven analytical approach, with framing from the perspectives of account sharing and privacy management. | Lampinen, A. (2014, February). Lampinen, A. (2016). |
| Hosting via the hospitality exchange platform Airbnb in Finland | 11 semi-structured interviews with altogether 12 participants who host guests via Airbnb. Material-driven analytical approach, with framing from the perspectives of hospitality and sociability. | Ikkala, T., and Lampinen, A. (2015, February). Ikkala, T., and Lampinen, A. (2014, February). |
| Hosting via the hospitality exchange platform Airbnb in the US | 12 semi-structured interviews with current, prior, or aspiring Airbnb hosts. Material-driven analytical approach, with framing from the perspectives of hospitality and social exchange theory. | Lampinen, A., and Cheshire, C. (2016, May). |

Methodologically, the empirical work featured in these case studies relies primarily on in-depth, semi-structured interviews, along with participant observation. To a lesser extent, some of the work on peer-to-peer exchange in local communities has involved elements of collaborative action research and co-design. The cases are situated in several settings, both in Finland and in the U.S., but it is worth noting that the research I draw upon is limited in its engagement with different communities and demographics. In particular, I want to note up front that most if not all participants across all cases have been white and relatively well-educated. This is crucial especially when it comes to the discussion of participation and inclusion where the voices represented are by and large the ones of those in a position to discriminate, wittingly or not, with little view into experiences of being discriminated against. Additionally, when it comes to the research on Airbnb, it is important to note that the hosts in these studies all considered hosting as a more or less casual, temporary, or supplementary form of income. Moreover, the studies featured both hosts engaged in *remote hospitality* (where the host is not physically sharing the home or other property he or she manages with the guest) and *on-site hospitality* (where the host is physically present and shares the apartment with the guest).

In writing this book, my aim has been to synthesize this set of case studies, re-analyzing the individual studies so as to arrange them under wider, overarching themes related to interpersonal challenges in peer-to-peer exchange. In doing so, I have also taken the opportunity to reflect on how things have evolved over time and what has become visible as the more persistent peer-to-peer exchange arrangements and platforms have had the time to mature. Here, I have benefited from re-visiting a fast-moving phenomenon—one that we were originally depicting just as it unfolded—at a time when the initial hype around the sharing economy has passed or at least started to fizzle out.

**Sidebox 1.1: Peer-to-peer exchange in local communities**

In Finland in 2008, we were at the beginnings of a large multidisciplinary research project called OtaSizzle that had the ambition to turn our university campus into a living lab for creating and studying mobile social services, and eventually enabling students and other community members to create their own services, too. One of the first services that the project team started to develop was focused on what we initially termed campus sourcing—taking the idea of crowdsourcing and situating it into the physical and social setting of a university campus, allowing people to reach out to the community via the service to have their needs met as well as to offer their help for others. Kassi was designed with the aim of linking those who can give something with those who are in need: Early on, the system was focused on the exchange of everyday favors such as borrowing items, sharing information, and helping other local community members in the course of daily life. Similar to online bulletin boards and classified advertisement systems like Craigslist, albeit designed specifically with a local community in mind, physical location and face-to-face interaction were often crucial in Kassi, since few exchanges could be completed solely online. Community members were free to offer and/or request as many favors, services and items as they liked.

There are two empirical cases related to the service that are central for this book: First, our research on the service in its original setting on our university campus in Finland (Lampinen et al., 2013; Suhonen et al., 2010), and second, a study of efforts to introduce the service for a single parents' network in the U.S. (Lampinen et al., 2015). Beyond the research itself, I have tracked the evolution of the system, originally named Kassi and later rebranded as Sharetribe, from its beginnings in the research project through to being spun off as a start-up and evolving in that form ever since. This has provided me with a valuable view into the sharing economy. From its roots as a platform for a particular local community, intent on enabling peer-to-peer exchange among community members, Sharetribe has changed markedly over the years and is now a company that provides software for others who wish to start multi-sided marketplaces. There is less of an emphasis now on community, gifting, and generalized exchange. Some of Sharetribe's customers still try out such models, while others are more strictly focused on monetary transacting.

**Sidebox 1.2: Hospitality exchange via Couchsurfing and Airbnb**

In the domain of platform-mediated hospitality, *network hospitality* is a term that seeks to capture how those engaging with hospitality exchange services connect to one another using online social networking systems, as well as to the kinds of relationships they perform when they meet face-to-face (Molz, 2014). Molz coined the term in discussing Couchsurfing, a system that facilitates non-monetary hospitality exchanges that rely on generalized reciprocity. It has since been applied also to monetary hospitality exchange, in particular Airbnb, the currently dominant platform for short-term rentals.

My research into this domain began with a project on multi-person households' experiences of hosting guests via Couchsurfing (Lampinen, 2016a, 2014) that I conducted while at Microsoft Research New England. After this crucial initial spark, two studies of Airbnb hosts followed: First, a project on hosts in Finland where I was fortunate to work with Tapio Ikkala (Ikkala and Lampinen, 2014, 2015), and second, a similar study in the U.S. with professor Coye Cheshire (Lampinen and Cheshire, 2016). None of these three cases were developed in collaboration with the respective companies, but I have since discussed findings from them with both Couchsurfing and Airbnb employees. Moreover, I have tracked the stories of both companies over the subsequent years in ways not captured in the original case studies. This has been influential for the ideas articulated in this book. Also, while I have never used Couchsurfing as a guest or a host, I have personal experiences of Airbnb as a guest and familiarity of the host perspective from having seen and discussed how friends and family have gone about hosting and reasoned around it. Echoing the point that the interpersonal can bear more weight than the technical, I have also plenty of personal experience of informal home sharing with more and less close friends, featuring the sometimes-awkward work around daring to ask, showing gratitude, avoiding indebtedness, and navigating hospitality in ways that aim to ensure relative comfort for all involved. I believe aspects of these experiences will be familiar to most readers even if they have never logged on to a hospitality exchange platform.

For the analysis in this book, my long-term involvement with the phenomenon has also been significant. I am writing as someone who started studying the sharing economy before the label became first popular and then problematic: When we first got started on peer-to-peer exchange, the idea of the sharing economy had yet to become popularized, even if ideas of community members helping one another or of people offering hospitality to strangers were of course not new as such. My understanding of what the sharing economy is and could be has been shaped by following the boom and bust of the term in both academic and popular writing, and by the role I have played a role in promoting peer-to-peer exchange as a domain worthy of scholarly attention. My involvement has meant continued attentiveness to the changing nature of what is happening empirically and required openness to reconsidering initial assumptions and ways of thinking in the face of new evidence and novel developments. I have followed developments in the sharing economy closely and I have personal experiences of the issues I write about but I have been neither a vocal advocate for the sharing economy nor a critical activist organizing against its harmful implications.

Given that I am trained as a social psychologist and a qualitative social scientist, it is perhaps not surprising that I am primed to argue for the importance of interpersonal aspects in making or breaking exchange arrangements. While my main interest has always been on what happens on the interpersonal level when individuals engage in peer-to-peer exchange (or fail or refuse to do so for various reasons), following the phenomenon closely has kept me attuned to organizational aspects such as how different initiatives can or cannot make it as businesses, the policy issues that bubble up, as well as the broader social and economic implications of peer-to-peer activities (or other activities self-identifying as part of a purported sharing economy). However, the analysis I provide does not focus on the legal and the economic issues with the sharing economy per se.

Working at the intersections of Human-Computer Interaction (and Computer-Supported Cooperative Work, CSCW, in particular) and the social sciences (Sociology, Anthropology, and Internet Research), I have also found it interesting and important to look for historical touchstones for the sharing economy. This book does not attempt to present original historical analysis, but, especially in Chapter 2, I turn to prior scholarship and recent literature reviews to trace some of the historical connections that underpin the sharing economy. Mapping out what is new and what is old pushes us to consider different elements of the sharing economy less as disruptive novelties and more on the historical continuums that they are part of.

## 1.4    WHY WE CAN'T HAVE NICE THINGS WITHOUT WORKING FOR THEM

This book is also motivated by the two-fold risk I see with current conversations about the sharing economy: First, venture-backed platforms prompt big headlines in mainstream media and capture a lot of the scholarly attention, to the point that we risk losing sight of all the community-led exchange arrangements that exist. These may be non-monetary and they are often local in their scope, typically intended to facilitate the co-use of resources in one form or another. Rather than always relying on a platform specifically designed to match the purpose, they may rely on digital technologies to a varying degree. Second, if we do not pay attention to such community-led action, it becomes difficult for us to support it with relevant research and suitable design interventions. In this way, the narrative of peers and communities getting sidelined turns into a self-fulfilling prophecy. In choosing to consider exchange arrangements where money plays little or no role, and understanding challenges involved in the social (and economic) encounters that they entail, we can open up important space for alternative arrangements and economies. Chapter 7 maps out future directions in this vein.

Setting aside common concerns about how requirements for scalability and profitability have hijacked the sharing economy, I believe we need to be frank about the interpersonal dynamics at play if we want to understand why so many peer-to-peer exchange arrangements fail to live up to their early promises. The interpersonal challenges this book focuses on pertain to exchange arrangements where those involved have some skin in the game and need to tackle social interactions alongside economic encounters. Alongside non-monetary and locally oriented arrangements, then, they are relevant also when money is changing hands as part of an exchange and even when money is a key driver of the exchange. In both cases, exchange partners may need to interact face-to-face with previously unfamiliar individuals or trust a stranger to come through with what was agreed upon when there are scarce assurances in place to guarantee that they will do so. For example, letting someone stay in one's home, be it for monetary compensation or not, holds the potential for closeness and vulnerability. As I will discuss in Chapter 6, this can be the case even when those regularly living in the apartment never meet those staying there temporarily.

### Sidebox 1.3: The trope of the power drill

If you have followed the story of the sharing economy, you are probably all too familiar with the trope about the power drill. Here's how it goes: Many people own a set of power tools that they use only seldomly. These risk obsolescence and, as they remain unused most of the time, can quickly feel like clutter that is taking place unnecessarily. So, the trope goes, wouldn't it be much better if neighbors would lend and borrow these from one another? People don't really want a drill, after all, they want to be able to make a small hole in the wall. Having only one set of seldom used power tools in an apartment block would be pragmatic: Less money and fewer natural resources spent to reach the same outcome, and perhaps in the process of sharing the local community would grow stronger, too! When sharing works out well, it leaves everyone feeling good: Most people love being able to help others, and when handled in a good way, learning to trust that it is ok to ask for help and rely on others in one's local community can feel equally good. Yet, in practice, even arrangements seemingly as simple as this often fail: Consumer goods are cheap enough for many to afford their own, and it is convenient to make small repairs whenever it suits us, without needing to reach out to a neighbor first. Hence, the benefit may simply not be big enough to warrant the effort. When things do not work out well, the mess that needs to get sorted can be more trouble than the upside could ever make up for.

The trope of the power drill (see Sidebox 1.3) illustrates well how we may love an idea while still finding it difficult to realize it in the midst of the unexpectedness and interconnectedness of everyday life. It is easy to romanticize neighborly relations and community spirit, but one thing that we have seen repeatedly in studies of peer-to-peer exchange is that many people are put off by the hassles of coordinating with others around them and the awkward dance of asking and offering, and then returning, thanking, and not-even-mentioning it. These challenges get more difficult when there is more at stake in the exchange than just an easily replaceable power tool. Organizing accommodation via systems like Airbnb and Couchsurfing has been one of the relative successes in the sharing economy. When it comes to sharing homes in this way, the exchange encounter is fraught in a way that picking up and dropping off a power drill typically is not. Exchange partners have to find ways to manage the three key challenges that this book focuses on: indebtedness, closeness, and participation. That can be difficult as all of these bring up risk and vulnerability which most people prefer to avoid. The good news is that when such exchanges work out well, they can provide wonderful experiences. The bad news is that to achieve such positive interpersonal outcomes, the exchange has to be a little difficult: Meaningful experiences of closeness come about when we overcome vulnerabilities, not by avoiding them altogether. The same goes for more locally oriented activities, such as participating in a time bank or making rarely used goods available to people in the neighborhood: it is not possible to buy community—the effort involved in doing things together is key for bringing about a sense of mutual care and building up capacities for continued cooperation (Light and Miskelly, 2019).

## 1.5    THE STRUCTURE OF THIS BOOK

Before diving into the interpersonal challenges that are at the heart of this book, Chapter 2 provides a brief mapping that situates **the sharing economy in its historical and contemporary context**. Chapter 3 offers a set of scoping questions that help in distinguishing phenomena that reside under the broad umbrella of the sharing economy. This is followed by chapters on the three key themes: Chapter 4 deals with **reciprocity and indebtedness**. Chapter 5 examines the social dynamics regarding **intimacy and closeness**. Finally, Chapter 6 explores how we might better address issues of **participation and inclusion**. Chapter 7 maps out **future directions**. It sums up lessons learned from a decade of research on peer-to-peer exchange, including supporting negotiations regarding reciprocity, allowing for social distance, and questioning face-to-face interaction as the gold standard for all exchange activities. Importantly, it also addresses how, despite early enthusiasm, the big story of peer-to-peer exchange arrangements seems to be one of failure. I call for both considering failures as a worthy object of study and revisiting our criteria of success. I close the book with an invitation to attend to the interpersonal issues that make peer-to-peer exchange so fraught for failure and yet so appealing.

## 1.6    INTENDED AUDIENCE

I have written this book with several audiences in mind. First, I hope it will help sustain scholarly interest—within and beyond the HCI and design communities—in the locally-oriented, peer-to-peer aspects of the sharing economy. I believe there is much work to do—not only in describing and documenting, but also intervening and generating. This book aims to encourage scholars to pursue these topics, be it by contributing to the agenda I propose or by pushing against it. Second, the book is designed to offer readers who are new to the scholarship on the sharing economy—in particular students at the Ph.D. and M.Sc. levels with both computer science and social science backgrounds—a thematic overview along with specific analytic footings that can help them in articulating their thoughts and identifying interesting projects to work on. Third, this book is also for practitioners and innovators hoping to initiate new peer-to-peer exchange arrangements. They may wish to skip over the more theoretical parts and focus on the pitfalls that the book documents and the lessons learned it offers for designing peer-to-peer exchange in a way that is sensitive to the interpersonal dynamics that can make or break an otherwise promising project.

## 1.7    WHAT IS OLD IS NEW AGAIN

Much of what has come to be known as the sharing economy was not always called the sharing economy. While claims of novelty and technological disruption have been abundant, on a closer look, it is often easy to see more continuity than change. It is not that there is nothing new about the sharing economy but many of the activities and initiatives involve communities and practices that date back much further in time than 2010 when visions of the sharing economy started to gain traction. To illustrate this with a concrete example, let us think for a moment of my childhood: I grew up on a farm in the Finnish countryside, in the same village where my father grew up before me. In my childhood, relying on neighbors and local networks was not the next big thing—it was simply how things got done. Similarly, co-ownership was not a disruptive innovation but rather a model people turned to where it made sense, often as an option taken in the absence of viable alternatives, with full knowledge that once you do not own something fully by yourself, you end up having to deal also with those you share it with, and you may not always agree with their views on how, when, and by whom the possession should be used and maintained. I was raised to believe that we are connected to those around us and rely on each other—and while this is, in my mind, a positive state of affairs, it was clear from very early on that one should not expect connection and reliance to be trouble-free and effortless. It takes effort to make relationships work, it isn't always easy to cooperate with those around you, and it certainly isn't always fun to navigate the treacherous terrain of asking and offering, giving and getting. It is this more down-to-earth, mundane side of the sharing economy that I believe holds some of the most interesting research problems and design challenges.

# CHAPTER 2

# Situating the Sharing Economy

*"[S]haring, both as a broad category of social practices,*
*and as the word used to describe a wide range of practices, is on the rise.*
*Ours is the age of sharing."*

— Nicholas A. John in *The Age of Sharing*

In his book *The Age of Sharing*, communications scholar Nicholas A. John (2017) argues that we live in the age of sharing: Today, there is a wide range of practices that are referred to as "sharing": these include posting updates on social network sites, or more generally the digital transfer of information; certain ways of exchanging goods and services; and talking about our emotions, or conveying information of affective import. John unpacks these three different but related spheres of sharing: sharing as the constitutive activity of social media; sharing as a model for economic behavior; and sharing as a category of speech. This book focuses on the second, but John's broader framing of the current uses of the word "sharing" is helpful for situating the sharing economy in a broader context. As John argues, while the three spheres are quite distinct and there may at first glance be little reason to bring them together, the metaphor of "sharing" is an important part of how practices in each are constructed and conceptualized. Moreover, when a practice is called "sharing," a certain stance between the participants is posited, involving values such as openness, trust, and maybe a sense of commonality (John, 2017). This rhetorical move is key to understanding why framing diverse activities as sharing has been so effective in making them sound attractive in the ears of broad audiences and how that has made it appealing for companies to market themselves as part of the sharing economy even when their platforms may have little to do with notions of gifts, favors, and community-mindedness that the term "sharing" tends to engender.

When the sharing economy made its entrance to the mainstream, there were ample claims of novelty, accompanied with a sense that technological innovation could facilitate a return to a romanticized past rich with co-use, gifting, and people helping one another. It is worth pausing to consider what is old and what is new: While the activities, technologies, and especially discourses characteristic of the sharing economy have novelty, practices of co-using and exchanging resources and efforts to connect communities with the help of digital technologies are, in and of themselves, not new. There are pre-existing forms of organizing that underlie them and longstanding social scientific theories that can help us understand them. The interpersonal challenges that have popped up in the context of online-mediated sharing are fundamental to social life. Over the past decade, as the sharing economy has become a domain of research within and beyond the field of Human–Computer Interaction (HCI), it has been tempting to focus on disruption rather than continuity in the social practices that are being facilitated and encouraged. Yet, both within HCI and outside it, there is a lot of relevant literature that predates the sharing economy and can inform us on many of the thorny challenges that we encounter anew in this emergent domain. As Dillahunt et al. (2017) have pointed out, paying attention to these pre-sharing economies allows us to shed light on the long-standing research questions that we re-encounter in studying the contemporary sharing economy.

In what follows, I will briefly situate the sharing economy in its historical and contemporary context: First, I will discuss the long histories of social exchange and hospitality as both social practices and topics of scholarly research. Second, I will depict how the sharing economy connects to platforms, marketplaces, and online communities. This brief mapping does not attempt to be, nor is it meant to be read as, an exhaustive account of the lineages and phenomena that the sharing economy is part of. Rather, it is intended to help us make sense of the sharing economy and, in particular, the empirical domains this book focuses on, as part of a historicized present.

## 2.1    SOCIAL EXCHANGE AND RECIPROCITY

Practices of gifting, sharing, and co-using resources predate the sharing economy, and we can trace scholarship on them back to early anthropological observations of exchange in societies. The most famous example is anthropologist Bronisław Malinowski's (1922/2014) classic ethnography on the Kula Ring: a stable exchange of decorative items with no real monetary value, but substantial symbolic value among the Trobriand Islanders of Papua New Guinea Sociologist and anthropologist Marcel Mauss (1925/2002) described this and other similar systems as gift economies, contrasting them with systems of bartering and negotiation. Malinowski's work became foundational for the social scientific study of reciprocity and exchange, and as such, it informs many scholarly efforts to make sense of peer-to-peer exchange.

Across different social, economic and anthropological perspectives, there is a key observation that individuals exchange goods and services through different forms of interaction, including gift giving, negotiation, and normative understandings of reciprocity. Mauss' distinction between gift economies and commodity (or market) economies is a point of interest also among contemporary scholars—and the tensions between these two types of economies remain unsettled. For example, anthropologist Anna Lowenhaupt Tsing's (2015, p. 122) ethnographic account of the Matsutake, depict mushrooms as both gifts and commodities, noting how *the contrast between gift and commodity suffers when it hits the ground; most situations juxtapose and confuse these ideal types—or stretch outside them.* This is the case also when it comes to the sharing economy: While it can be tempting to separate monetary modes of exchange neatly from the non-monetary, the distinction is rarely that straightforward.

As online peer-to-peer exchange systems involve the transfer of valued resources—such as access to physical spaces and the comforts that come with it—between parties who have likely never met face-to-face before, it brings about both economic and social outcomes. Social exchange theory is one sociological tradition that can help us make sense of the issues we encounter in the sharing economy. According to social exchange theory, social exchange is a fundamental human activity that helps to explain social behavior through the process of exchanging valued goods and services (Blau, 1986). It is vital to social interaction. As Cook and Emerson (1978) argue, beyond the material value of exchange, participation in systems of social exchange can produce social value for participants and for communities as a whole, including commitment, emotional attachment, and solidarity. We rely on norms and institutions to live together.

Social exchange theory distinguishes between negotiated, reciprocal, and generalized exchange: *Negotiated exchange* is a form of direct exchange that occurs when two individuals bargain and discuss the terms of an agreement before exchanging goods or services (Cook and Emerson, 1984; Lawler and Yoon, 1993). *Reciprocal exchange* does not involve any explicit agreement between parties, but the exchange of goods and services still takes place directly between two individuals (Molm, 1988, 1997). *Generalized exchange* is an indirect form of exchange—there are no direct agreements or negotiations. It refers to acts of indirect reciprocity in the form of either collective goods where individuals contribute to an outcome that benefits many or networks of indirect gifts and favors where the providers rarely receive benefits from the same recipients (Ekeh, 1974; Yamagishi and Cook, 1993).

While all three types of exchange feature in the sharing economy, let us consider in generalized exchange in more detail as it is likely the least familiar if them for most people: The hospitality exchange community Couchsurfing is an example of a type of generalized exchange referred to as *network-generalized exchange* (Ekeh, 1974; Yamagishi and Cook, 1993): It occurs when individuals give to one person but the recipient gives to someone else, continuing ad infinitum in a large chain or network of unilateral gift-giving. Here, a gift received does not imply an expectation of reciprocity with the same person in the future. Another type of generalized exchange occurs when individuals contribute goods and services towards a collective effort, which is then redistributed as a reward to the entire community. Ekeh (1974) calls this type of exchange *group-generalized exchange* since the group acts as the indirect third party between individual contributors and recipients. The problem of maintaining a clean kitchen in a shared house is an example of group-generalized exchange since each person may or may not clean, but everyone benefits from the pooled efforts of those who do (Yamagishi and Cook, 1993). In online environments, pooled contributions of information often take the form of group-generalized exchange (Cheshire, 2007). Examples of such information pools (Cheshire and Antin, 2008, 2009) include peer-to-peer file sharing networks, open-source software projects, multimedia contribution sites, and public online forums.

Different forms of exchange impose different levels of risk and uncertainty on those involved. In peer-to-peer exchange, individuals may face many sources of uncertainty. One source of uncertainty arises when decisions are made with new, unknown individuals instead of fixed partners (Cook et al., 2005). Social research on trust-building processes demonstrates that trust typically develops in a gradual way as individuals take small risks with one another, and slowly increase the amount of risk over time (Cook et al., 2005). The basis for taking risks is the hope that someone will honor the trust placed in them. While people may cooperate with one another based merely on the expectation or hope that the exchange partner will reciprocate and fulfill agreed-upon obligations, they develop trust only over time when cooperation is achieved, after they have experienced the person following through on promises and obligations. This means that trust is more likely to develop when it comes to repeated exchange with the same partner rather than one-off encounters. However, the presence of a third-party assurance structure can reduce the need for interpersonal trust between the two primary parties (Cook et al., 2009): two individuals do not need to trust one another to fulfill an agreement if they can rely entirely on the assurance structure to guarantee the transaction. This is why assurance structures may make it possible for individuals who are risk-averse or generally more cautious of others to take an initial leap of faith by interacting with unfamiliar exchange partners (Cook et al., 2009).

Finally, in Emerson's early formulation of social exchange theory, reciprocity is the foundation of exchange (Emerson, 1972a, 1972b): norms of obligation emerge to reinforce reciprocity and they are needed for sustaining exchange arrangements. While this book draws upon social exchange theory to make sense of peer-to-peer exchange, it is worth noting that others have approached sharing with different conceptual lenses. Most importantly, Belk (2010) distinguishes non-ownership-based sharing from gift giving and commodity exchange. Further, he argues that the non-reciprocal nature of sharing is, in fact, one of the characteristics that sets it apart from gift-giving and commodity exchange.

## 2.2    HOSPITALITY AND SOCIABLE ENCOUNTERS

In defining hospitality in terms of exchange, hospitality scholar Bob Brotherton (1999) emphasizes the relationship between the host and the guest, the two fundamental parties in hospitality. He frames hospitality as an exchange that incorporates both material and symbolic transactions, including offering accommodation, food, drink, and expressions of gratitude. Arguing from an anthropological point of view, Selwyn (2013) states that hospitality can be seen as a fundamental form of social interaction that establishes solidarity and feelings of togetherness between people. Acts of hospitality establish and consolidate links between individuals and groups; thereby, hospitality is an important social form holding societies together (Selwyn, 2013). Hospitality can be either conditional or unconditional; that is, it can be acted out for purposes of making a profit or be offered without any expectation of compensation from the receiving party (Morrison and O'Gorman, 2006).

The platform-based hospitality phenomenon that Couchsurfing and Airbnb are part of is still relatively recent. Communication scholar Jennie Germann Molz has coined the term *network hospitality* to refer to the way users of hospitality exchange services "*connect to one another using online social networking systems, as well as to the kinds of relationships they perform when they meet each other offline and face to face*" (Molz, 2014, 2012). Bialski (2012a, p. 44–5) argues that host–guest interaction in network hospitality can be conceived of as a form of sociability: a form of association into which people enter for the sake of "*the sheer pleasure of the company of others*." It is notable that hospitality is often understood to go beyond its material aspects: the social interaction between the host(s) and the guest(s) is an important aspect of how hospitality plays out. It is when we view hospitality from this point of view, that sociologist Georg Simmel's (1903/1950) classic idea of sociability becomes relevant: Sociability gains its value from interaction in its own right, rather than some ulterior motive or a practical purpose. It is "*homogenic interaction*" in which participants are expected to act as if all interacting parties were equal and genuinely equally respected. Moreover, the contents of the sociable "chat" have to be interesting for all participants, in order to allow for a lively exchange of talk. These requirements explain, in part, why it can be easiest to accomplish sociable interaction with people who are similar to oneself in social standing, interests, and favored codes of interaction.

Extending hospitality to strangers is, of course, no novelty. Network hospitality sites and services are the latest link in a long lineage of attempts to "burst the tourist bubble" by replacing traditional commercial intermediaries, such as hotels and by facilitating peer-to-peer connections between travelers and locals (Lampinen, 2016). While Molz' definition centers the role of networked technologies in hospitality exchange, it is useful to consider in brief how the tradition of organized hospitality exchange predates the emergence of such systems. Scholars in tourism and hospitality studies have documented various formal and informal hospitality networks through which people provided meals, transportation, accommodation, or other aid for traveling strangers. For example, Adler's (1985) historical analysis of tramping describes how trade societies established networks of homes and inns to accommodate traveling craftsmen in early nineteenth-century England. Before broader availability of internet connectivity, people relied on telephone calls, letters, and postcards to arrange homestays around the world (Molz, 2012). As one example of a more formalized network, SERVAS International, a non-profit cooperative, was founded after World War II to coordinate hospitality exchange, with the underlying aim to promote tolerance and world peace through person-to-person interactions (Molz, 2012). In the 1990s, SERVAS' printed lists became obsolete in sync with the emergence of online networks, including Hospitality Club, Global Freeloaders, Hospitality Exchange and, eventually, Couchsurfing (Molz, 2012).

In addition to acknowledging the long history of hospitality exchange arrangements, it is also worth remembering that despite what mainstream media accounts might lead us to assume, the rise of commercial systems like Airbnb has not fully crowded out other, non-monetary forms of network hospitality: Palgan, Zvolska, and Mont (2017) argue against treating accommodation sharing as a homogeneous sector and offer a categorization that divides services into rental, reciprocal, and free platforms. Here, *reciprocal platforms* refer to services involving home swapping, while services often considered as running on a generalized reciprocity arrangement, such as Couchsurfing, are categorized as *free*. As Ferreira et al. (2019) highlight in a study on long-distance cycling, Couchsurfing is still actively used and there are also further, lesser known networks, such as WarmShowers that is maintained by and for the cycling community, that operate as gift economies.

## 2.3    ONLINE MARKETPLACES AND EXCHANGE PLATFORMS

Town squares and market halls are two familiar examples of *marketplaces*: venues where supply and demand meet. Nowadays, it is common for markets to be implemented by creating a marketplace using a computer system (Hosio et al., 2014)—and different internet-based marketplaces are now some of the world's biggest and fastest-growing businesses (Roth, 2015). Over the past couple of decades, online marketplaces have grown in their influence, complexity, and scope. While originally limited to the exchange of physical goods, such as on eBay, exchange platforms are increasingly used to transact services, too, such as transport via Uber or accommodation via Airbnb. Within HCI, markets have been deployed and studied, for instance, in the domains of auctions and commodity markets (Resnick et al., 2000; Resnick and Zeckhauser, 2002), community commerce via Facebook (Moser et al., 2017), as well as game markets and virtual economies (Lehdonvirta and Castronova, 2014). Further studies have considered peer-to-peer exchange systems like Craigslist (Lingel, 2020) and business-to-business markets (Kollock and Braziel, 2006).

Markets are a diverse phenomenon and they can take on many forms, some of which challenge our conventional understandings of what markets are, and some in which money plays little to no role (Roth, 2015). Regardless of the role of money, when it comes to the sharing economy, we are typically dealing with *two-sided markets* where there are numerous actors on both sides of the market. For example, on Airbnb and other hospitality platforms there are many hosts being matched with many guests. In particular, the markets in peer-to-peer exchange are often *matching markets*, that is, markets where money is not the only determinant of who gets what, where the participants care, sometimes deeply, about who they are dealing with, and where the market involves searching and wooing on both sides (Roth, 2015). Think, for example, of Couchsurfing hosts and guests, both of whom want to ensure that an exchange they commit to works for them. When guests and hosts spend time together in person, both typically have an interest in who they match with. This is quite different from the common, classic definition of a market as the interaction of supply and demand for a particular good or service resulting in exchange (Lehdonvirta and Castronova, 2014). Yet, much like the distinction between gift and commodity economies, the line between *"perfectly anonymous commodity markets and relationship-specific matching markets"* is not clear-cut—the conceptualization is better thought of as a spectrum from pure commodity to pure matching (Roth, 2015). Part of what can make the sharing economy so controversial is the ambiguity of its placement on this spectrum and the fact that different exchange arrangements are geared for different types of exchange—and even within one particular exchange arrangement those involved may seek to participate based on differing understandings and preferences.

In situating the sharing economy, it is worthwhile to dwell briefly on the notion of *platforms*. The term holds many different meanings, ranging from the computational to the architectural, figurative, and political (Gillespie, 2010). While platforms were initially understood in the computational sense as infrastructures that support the design and use of particular applications and as online environments that allow users to design and deploy applications they design or are offered by third parties, over time there has been a shift from the technical to a socio-technical focus: Platforms are recognized as such not because they allow code to be written or run, but because they afford an opportunity to communicate, interact, or sell (Gillespie, 2010). It is this newer meaning that makes talking about platforms sensible when it comes to online-mediated peer-to-peer exchange.

Platforms shape the interactional space available for those involved in them (Ilten, 2015). Exchange platforms (or rather, those in charge of them) are not powerless to make value choices and shape the outcomes among those who exchange on the market that they have created. Sometimes, platforms provide assurances that facilitate peer-to-peer encounters and make interpersonal interaction smoother (Lampinen and Cheshire, 2016): First, structured, platform-managed payment processes provide convenience and increased reliability of payment, thereby removing uncertainty and alleviating awkwardness on both sides of the market. These paymentless payments have been observed to be important also in gig work systems, such as Uber (Glöss et al., 2016). In this context, while convenient for the customers, they may involve problems for service providers, for instance, by doing away with established practices of tipping that workers rely on as a part of their income (Raval and Dourish, 2016). Second, platform companies can also step in to help to resolve conflicts between exchange partners. In these instances, the platform company is called upon to act as an authoritative, third-party mediator who supports and confirms the binding nature of the peer-to-peer exchange and helps resolve conflicts between hosts and guests. Platforms, if they take on that responsibility, can play a crucial role in supporting exchange encounters both by making interactions less awkward and by helping when things go wrong—but providing assurance structures requires significant resources, and different services may be more or less willing and capable to invest in them.

While crowdsourcing and gig work are beyond the scope of this book, they are a central part of the broader contemporary landscape of online marketplaces and exchange platforms. First, it is worth noting that on-demand labor systems do not constitute historically unprecedented logics of arranging labor. Rather, they are a contemporary form of piecework (Alkhatib et al., 2017; Dubal, 2020; Lehdonvirta, 2018) and the word gig relates them directly to how musicians' labor has long been organized (Baym, 2018). Second, in response to concerns over the shape that platform labor is taking, there have been efforts to create more equitable and inclusive forms of organizing, such as *cooperatives* and other *social enterprises* (Orsi, 2014; Scholz, 2017). In their focus on rethinking structures of governance and ownership, these have the potential to inform how a variety of sharing economies might organize differently. Particularly noteworthy is *platform cooperativism*, an emerging movement for rethinking platform-mediated work so as to benefit workers and their local communities. The movement builds on the long tradition of cooperative organizing. As Scholz and Schneider (2017, p. 11) put it, the goal of platform cooperativism is to find (and bring about) "*an optimistic vision for the future of work and life*"—as an alternative to exploitations and abuses identified in the status quo—by "*considering the emerging platforms in light of well-hewn cooperative principles and practices,*" most importantly the tenets of communal ownership and democratic governance. Platform cooperativism is a good example of the enthusiasm there is to consider how lessons learned from the long history of cooperatives could expand our thinking of what future economies can look like and the roles technologies may play in them, and, on the other hand, how contemporary and future technologies could be harnessed to tackle some of the problems distinct to member-owned alternative forms of organizing (Lampinen et al., 2018).

## 2.4   ONLINE COMMUNITIES AND COMMUNITY INFORMATICS

Finally, in tracing the roots of the sharing economy, connections to both online and offline communities are one obvious area to consider. Research that considers the internet as an enabler of new form of technologically enabled social life goes back several decades at this point (Turner, 2005): For just a few examples, consider communication scholar Nancy Baym's (1995, 2000) research on an online fan community or freelance journalist Howard Rheingold's (1993) early writings about *virtual community*.

As Mosconi et al. (2017) note in writing about Facebook as a neighborhood technology, while the internet can be powerful in connecting those who live far apart, it is equally common that digital technologies are used to support socializing among people with close social ties and those who live in the same area. In many ways, this has always been the case: Even Rheingold's original virtual community—WELL, the San Francisco Bay Area bulletin-board system known as the Whole Earth 'Lectronic Link—was in many ways shaped by and local to the Bay Area, despite acting also "*a medium through which geographically dispersed members of separate networks could write to one another, create a textual record of their interaction, and so begin to build a sense of shared consciousness and collectivity.*" And even here, the co-existence of sociality and economic activity is always already part of the story (Turner, 2005, p. 499). This resonates with John's (2017) apt observation that the term sharing gets used in relation to both posting updates on social network sites, or more generally the digital transfer of information, and certain ways of exchanging goods and services.

Articulating a broader research program regarding the role of ICTs in community life, Gurstein (2007, p. 11) has defined *community informatics* as "the application of information and communications technology (ICT) to enable and empower community processes." Here, community informatics is understood to work from the assumption that geographically local communities have distinct characteristics, requirements, and opportunities, and that, in turn, it is necessary to tailor strategies for ICT intervention and development accordingly to match them. In CSCW and HCI, too, the role of information and communication technologies in community and civic organizations has long been a domain of interest, including through the development of approaches to participatory design (Bannon and Ehn, 2012; Muller, 2007) and the more recent focus on civic technologies (Boehner and DiSalvo, 2016; Pilemalm, 2018; Vlachokyriakos et al., 2016). Scholars have recognized local community life as a rich context for understanding challenges and possibilities of information technology (Carroll and Rosson, 2013). Researchers have sought to study communities and design technologies for them in ways that go beyond a naïve celebration of the vague social goodness that gets ascribed to a group when it is referred to as a community (Carroll, 2014). These approaches and critiques are worth revisiting in thinking about peer-to-peer exchange since *sharing* shares many of these discursive challenges with *community*: when it comes to sharing, practices on the ground are much more complicated and interesting than the surface-level connotations might lead us to assume.

Much of the research in HCI on local and civic initiatives relies on the idea that citizens can affect change in their own communities (Mair et al., 2006). While these efforts can entail entirely new, locally tailored community technologies, global sites like Facebook are commonly used for engaging with the places where people live and the local issues they face: citizens appropriate technologies with global reach to serve local ends (Mosconi et al., 2017). Lambton-Howard et al. (2020) have labeled this approach as *unplatformed design*. While the sharing economy is often associated with big platforms, a mixture of bespoke platforms and needs-driven constellations of commonly available technologies has been characteristic of the many *self-organizing sharing initiatives* that researchers have documented over the past decade. As just a small glimpse to the varied efforts to support local arrangements of peer-to-peer exchange and co-use of resources, we may think of food sharing (Berns et al., 2021a, 2021b; Ganglbauer et al., 2014), time banks (Bellotti et al., 2015, 2014; Seyfang and Smith, 2002), tool libraries (Fedosov et al., 2018) and further, more broadly scoped systems that are meant to help people exchange goods and services within their local community (Fedosov et al., 2021; Lampinen et al., 2015; Light and Miskelly, 2015; Suhonen et al., 2010).

CHAPTER 3

# What Do We Talk About When We Talk About the Sharing Economy?

*"Nonprofits have been part of the story since the beginning,*
*and to write them out helps foreclose the future they are working toward.*
*That aspiration is also why we continue to use the term sharing,*
*despite the many ways in which "Big Sharing" platforms are violating its meaning."*

— Juliet B. Schor in *After the Gig*

What do we talk about when we talk about the sharing economy? Sharing economy is a broad umbrella term, and it gets used to refer to such a range of disparate activities and arrangements that, on its own, it is of scarce analytical use. Over time, I have become less and less convinced that striving for a singular definition of the sharing economy is meaningful or that having one would even be particularly productive for advancing research and design. As an alternative path forward, this chapter provides a set of scoping questions. These are intended to facilitate productive conversations or, at least, help us be more precise about what exactly we are talking about and avoid getting bogged down in arguments about terminology. My aim is not to propose criteria for distinguishing "real sharing" from "fake"—or community-minded nonprofits from "Big Sharing" platforms, for that matter. Instead, the questions are meant to serve as tools for thinking and discussion.

The seven questions offer lenses through which we can scrutinize different aspects of the purported sharing economy. There is purposeful overlap between the questions: they consider closely related issues with slightly different framings, with the hope that one or another will make it easier to characterize and unpack any particular phenomenon. The questions map loosely onto the three interpersonal challenges at the heart of this book: In helping us make distinctions between different types of peer-to-peer exchange, they shed light on modes of reciprocation, the potential for closeness and intimacy, as well as issues of participation and the power to shape how and between whom sharing happens.

1. **What is being exchanged?**

Let us start from the premise that everything that gets characterized as part of the sharing economy has to do with some kind of exchange. This alone does not tell us much—understood in a broad sense, what an exchange is might range from buying a service or swapping one item for another, to doing another person a favor in hopes that they will pay it forward. So, the first question asks *what is it that is being exchanged*.

One key distinction we can make in the sharing economy is whether an exchange has to do primarily with *labor* or *assets*: Some exchange arrangements are about different types of assets, be it making an apartment available for visitors or lending physical goods among neighbors. Others are more fairly characterized as having to do with labor, such as paid services like the on-demand taxi companies Uber and Lyft but also other types of arrangements like timebanks where human effort is central to the exchange. The question asks about the primary focus of the exchange, since labor and assets are not always easily separable. Think, for instance, of an Airbnb rental where a room or an apartment (or other accommodation) is the object of exchange. While the asset here is clearly crucial for the exchange, there is also significant labor involved in hosting via Airbnb—and this may range from offering hospitality occasionally in one's home to hosting practices that are best understood as professionalized short-term rentals, akin to running a hotel.

To simplify, we can identify two distinct phenomena that are often referenced under the umbrella of the sharing economy: *peer-to-peer exchange* and *on-demand labor*. While many prefer to exclude on-demand labor (also referred to as gig work or the gig economy) from the sharing economy, it keeps coming up and confounding discussions about the sharing economy. To avoid an argument every time that happens, it is more effective to scope down the discussion by using a more precise term (peer-to-peer exchange vs on-demand labor).

**2. How do those involved reciprocate? What is the role of money?**

The second question is closely connected with the first: How do those involved reciprocate? All exchange arrangements need some *mechanism(s) for reciprocation*, be it monetary transactions or either direct or generalized gifting. The most familiar form is *direct reciprocity* where those making the exchange even things out with one another. *Generalized reciprocity* functions on the level of a community (and over time), such as in Couchsurfing where guests are expected to "pay back" the hospitality they have received by hosting visitors in their homes or contributing to the community in some other way.

This question also prompts us to consider *the role of money in the exchange*. Exchanging like for like is an exception with most contemporary economies, while trading goods or services for money tends to be the norm. In contrast, it might seem tempting to exclude all monetary exchange when it comes to the sharing economy—after all, why call it sharing if it is better understood as transacting? An empirically grounded approach invites us to acknowledge both that money is commonly used in activities that are labeled as part of the sharing economy and, more importantly, that the presence of money does not foreclose the possibility of other parallel types of reciprocity that better reflect the kinds of efforts and affects that resonate with common understandings of sharing. Chapter 4 will dive deeper into these issues.

3.  **How common is it for those involved to take part on both sides of the market?**

Borrowing from economics, it is often helpful to conceptualize exchange in the sharing economy as a two-sided market, that is, an arrangement typically established and enabled by a digital platform that brings together two groups of actors (e.g., hosts and guests, or service providers and customers). With this framing, we can ask how common it is for those involved to participate on both sides of the market. Is it typical for participants on each side of the market to swap roles or do people tend to participate always in the same capacity? Relating to the previous question, this continues to unpack the role of money in exchange arrangements, since when *roles on each side of the market* are more specialized, it is more likely that reciprocation involves a monetary element. The level to which roles are differentiated has implications for the potential (and appropriateness) of closeness and intimacy.

The question serves as something of a litmus test for distinguishing between gig work and peer-to-peer exchange. For instance, in a time bank, the expectation is that all participants both give and receive help. The whole arrangement relies on that type of reciprocity. This, then, can be taken as a straightforward example of peer-to-peer exchange. On the other hand, when it comes to taxi services like Uber, it is less likely that a passenger will also work as a driver. Here, the roles of the exchange partners are better described as those of a service provider and a customer. This gives us reason to classify such services as on-demand labor. As a third example, we can think of a service like Airbnb and how it has evolved over time. Here, we can expect to find more participants acting on both sides of the market—at least in the sense that many hosts occasionally participate also as guests. Over time, though, the trend in Airbnb seems to have been toward increasing separation of the roles of hosts and guests. This illustrates how the question can help us consider particular exchange arrangements over time, in addition to making distinctions between different instances of sharing.

4. **How do the exchange partners interact with one another?**

Beyond the roles of different participants, we may also ask *how much the exchange partners interact with one another—and in what way*. Exchange arrangements differ in the kinds of face-to-face encounters they necessitate or encourage as well as the extent to which exchange partners interact with one another online. As will be discussed in Chapter 5, the amount and mode of interaction between exchange partners comes up in (moral) assessments of whether different activities can meaningfully be characterized as part of a sharing economy. However, the objective with this question is not to classify different types of exchange as more or less credible examples of the sharing economy or to make value judgements, but rather to help us narrow in on the interactional character of the exchange. The demands on participants—and on any supportive technologies—differ depending on what kind of an exchange process they are navigating. This has implications for how much of a need (or opportunity) participants have for establishing interpersonal trust, how much it matters who they interact with, and what they can expect from the exchange by way of sociability and relationship building.

5. **Who can participate?**

Priming us for the discussion on participation and inclusion in Chapter 6, another question that can guide our understanding of the sharing economy is *who can participate*. Even if the initial answer to this is often "anyone who would like," upon closer inspection, we may find structures and dynamics that make it impossible or at least highly unlikely that everyone really is in a position to participate if they so choose. We may also probe further by asking how easily different people can get involved—and of course, especially when it comes to exchange arrangements that have been around for a while, it is worth asking *who does participate* to understand how things are playing out in practice. In considering this question, we may learn uncomfortable lessons. As Schor (2020) has documented, well-meaning initiatives may fall short on their promises or even end up amplifying the very differences that they were hoping to bridge: instead of succeeding in offering an alternative to aspects of the conventional economy, such as race, class, and gender exclusion, many community-based start-ups found themselves reproducing the same dynamics. Taking a more expansive view, we may also ask who can participate in setting rules for the sharing economy as well as consider who is affected by the sharing economy. This is important for ensuring that consideration is given to people who do not wish to engage in exchanges but are affected by them, such as neighbours of Airbnb units—an issue we will revisit in more detail in Chapter 6.

6. **What (if any) is the role of digital technologies?**

Rather than assuming that a digital platform always plays a central role, it is worth considering explicitly whether digital technologies are part of the exchange arrangement—and if yes, what kinds of technologies are they and what is their role and purpose? Many exchange arrangements are structured, enabled, and constrained by a central technology. Relating to the aforementioned question of who gets to set the rules, while platforms can dictate to a large extent how the two sides of a market come together, they may also leave details largely up to the participants themselves, providing scarce guidance on how to participate. Beyond platforms, some exchange arrangements rely on commonly available tools like the social network site Facebook or the instant messaging service WhatsApp while others have overall very little to do with digital technologies. For example, neighborly peer-to-peer exchange, especially the gifting away of used goods, might be facilitated with an old-fashioned notice board or a dedicated physical location, such as a windowsill in the stairwell of an apartment building or a table in the lobby of the local library branch. Where the exchange arrangement is not structured around a specific technology, there is a lot to be learned by attending to the constellations of technologies that participants have put in place to facilitate their activities—and here, again, we may ask who has made the choices of which tools to use and who has the power to make changes to the constellation.

7. **What aspirations are there related to the exchange arrangement?**

The final question invites reflection *aspirations related to the exchange arrangement.* Why does the arrangement exist? Who benefits from it? Who is harmed by it? Here, we can try to separate out the aspirations of those engaging in exchange, those in charge of the arrangement (be it owners of a platform or community organizers), and perhaps also those not directly involved yet impacted by the arrangement. Whether an exchange arrangement is set up as a company or a community initiative has important implications to how it is run and what we can expect from it, both in terms of the kinds of activities it is geared to promote and the resources available for advancing desired outcomes. Exchange arrangements differ, for example, in the kinds of relational experiences as well as environmental and economic outcomes that they are designed to advance. Sometimes interpersonal encounters are at the heart of why an initiative exists, in other cases requirements for in-person interactions register rather as a necessary evil. Some arrangements are driven by the pursuit of monetary profits, while others are more focused on community-building or sustainability. It is also always worth asking whose aspirations are factored in when decisions about future directions are made or the choice is made to foster one value at the cost of another. I will return to these questions regarding design, values, and design ethics in the final sections of the book.

CHAPTER 4

# Reciprocity and Indebtedness

*"Asking for help with shame says:*
*You have the power over me.*
*Asking with condescension says:*
*I have the power over you.*
*But asking for help with gratitude says:*
*We have the power to help each other."*

— Amanda Palmer in *The Art of Asking*

Social exchanges are vital to social interaction. They are a core part of romantic relationships and friendships, barters and negotiations, favors and gifts. *The norm of reciprocity* is a central aspect of social exchange: Simply put, individuals tend to feel a sense of responsibility after someone provides a gift or another act of kindness (Gouldner, 1960). Yet, it would be a mistake to focus solely on what happens after receiving a kindness: it is also common for individuals to struggle with asking for help or to be reluctant to accept it even when offered, either in anticipation of the negative feelings associated with debts of gratitude and/or because it would conflict with their striving for self-sufficiency. As the quote from singer-songwriter Amanda Palmer's (2014) bestselling book illustrates, the social dynamics of asking for, giving, and receiving help are fraught. Participation in these exchange activities is a skilled social accomplishment (see Chapter 2 for classic anthropological observations of gift exchange). There is a reason it is called *the art of asking*.

Dealing with *reciprocity* and the closely related issue of *indebtedness*, then, should be a crucial concern for any socio-technical system designed to facilitate and encourage social exchange. As most people know from personal experience, asking for help can feel difficult and uncomfortable. Having to express that one needs help can evoke feelings of shame and embarrassment. The desire to be—or at least appear—self-sufficient is strong. Beyond the expected awkwardness of asking for help, an aversion to indebtedness may lead potential exchange partners to be unwilling to accept gifts or help, especially if they do not expect to be capable of reciprocation in the future. Feeling stuck with a debt of gratitude is something many people would rather avoid.

This chapter dives into different forms of exchange and the layers of reciprocity that are necessary for the functioning of peer-to-peer exchange. Sidebox 4.1 provides a brief overview of the different, direct and indirect, forms of social exchange. While we can approach social exchange analytically with distinct theoretical categories, in practice different forms of exchange are often intertwined. To illustrate the interpersonal challenges that reciprocity poses, this chapter features two examples: The first is Kassi—the early peer-to-peer exchange system introduced in Chapter 1—and, in particular, its use in a Finnish student community.[1] Drawing on our research team's experiences, I discuss how fears of indebtedness can be a deterrent to peer-to-peer exchange, in parallel to (or even more so than) fears regarding freeriding. The second case concerns short-term accommodation via Couchsurfing and Airbnb and illustrates how different forms of exchange intertwine.[2] Here, I argue that even when money is an obvious and effective means for balancing out an exchange, it alone is often not enough for peer-to-peer exchange to unfold in a satisfactory—or enjoyable—manner.

### Sidebox 4.1: Direct and indirect forms of social exchange

**Social exchange** is a fundamental human activity that helps to explain social behavior through the process of exchanging valued goods and services (Blau, 1986). Beyond the basic starting point of transferring valued resources or carrying out mutually rewarding actions, the *form of an exchange* is crucial for the experience of participating in an exchange and the outcomes of the exchange. There are three major types of social exchange: negotiated, reciprocal, and generalized exchange (Cheshire et al., 2010).

**Negotiated exchange** is a form of direct exchange that occurs when two individuals bargain and discuss the terms of an agreement before exchanging goods or services (Cook and Emerson, 1984; Lawler and Yoon, 1993). For example, buyers and sellers who barter after connecting through an online classified advert, such as a listing on Craigslist, engage in online negotiated exchange (Willer et al., 2012). Negotiated exchange tends to include economic exchanges such as bargaining and prior agreements on trades or purchases. Binding negotiated exchanges involve direct negotiation of valued resources with very little uncertainty about agreed outcomes Cheshire et al., 2010).

---

[1]  This section draws on co-authored research previously published in Lampinen et al. (2013) and Suhonen et al. (2010).

[2]  This section draws on research previously published in Ikkala and Lampinen (2014; 2015), Lampinen (2014, 2016), and Lampinen and Cheshire (2016).

**Reciprocal exchange** is another form of direct exchange. It does not involve any explicit agreement between parties, but the exchange of goods and services still takes place directly between two individuals (Molm, 1988, 1997). Reciprocal exchange includes direct reciprocity such as gifts or favors that are sometimes repaid, but lacks any terms or agreements such as those in negotiated exchange. When exchange relies on implicit expectations based on the norm of reciprocity, rather than explicit agreements, it is highly uncertain. For example, a reciprocal exchange occurs when an individual borrows something from another person and then returns the favor to the same person at a later time. At the time of the first exchange, however, there are no formal assurances in place that the favor will ever be returned.

**Generalized exchange** is an indirect form of exchange—there are no direct agreements or negotiations. It refers to acts of indirect reciprocity in the form of either *collective goods* where individuals contribute to an outcome that benefits many or *networks of indirect gifts and favors* where the providers rarely receive benefits from the same recipients (Ekeh, 1974; Yamagishi and Cook, 1993). In other words, individuals provide resources of some form to an actor or group, and the recipient(s) may or may not provide resources to others in the future. When individuals engage in generalized exchange, they provide valued resources to others with no expectation of direct reciprocity (a repayment or benefit from the same person) (Yamagishi and Cook, 1993). One example of generalized exchange is Couchsurfing: Guests are not expected to compensate hosts directly for the hospitality they receive. Instead, the expectation is that the guests will "pay it forward" by providing hospitality to somebody else in the future. Generalized exchange is often used interchangeably with terms such as gift economies, gift exchange, and generalized reciprocity (Ekeh, 1974).

## 4.1    NEGOTIATING RECIPROCITY AND DEALING WITH FEARS OF INDEBTEDNESS

Back in 2008, our research project team at Aalto University in Finland started working on the early version of the peer-to-peer exchange system Kassi. In debating the design of the system and in planning for how to study its uses and non-uses once it was made available for the university community, concerns about freeriding were voiced regularly. Would unscrupulous community members take advantage of those making kind offers on the site? Was there any reason to hope that the system would work over time if we did not implement strict protocols for reciprocation or obligatory reviews that would ensure sturdy reputation mechanisms? Some felt it would be necessary to introduce some kind of currency into the system. Yet others worried that if we were to launch a currency, we would need to have mechanisms to prevent speculation and artificial inflation. Evidently, the only way to really find out what would happen was to let community members try out the system.

In 2010, we described the challenge with local peer-to-peer exchange systems in this way: "*We all have skills and possessions that others need but do not have. At the same time, we often lack items or skills ourselves, and seek others who can help. Even from a close friend, but perhaps especially from a stranger, it does not always come naturally to ask for a favor. Often there is a gap between what any one individual has or can do and what he is willing to ask for from others*" (Suhonen et al., 2010). Kassi sought to tackle these issues with a focus on the exchange of everyday favors such as borrowing items, sharing information, and helping other local community members in the course of daily life. Similar to online bulletin boards and classified advertisement systems like Craigslist, albeit designed specifically for the local community on our university campus, physical location and face-to-face interaction were often crucial: few exchanges could be completed solely online.

Kassi did not encourage haggling over prices, and there was no functionality for bidding on goods or services—or for paying for them. The service was designed to support direct communication to allow all forms of exchange without implying any particular type of interaction such as negotiation or gifting. For instance, participants were free to decide how they wanted to offer or request goods and services. The system was agnostic about suitable forms of exchange and the possible role of money in them, leaving it up to the community members to figure it out for themselves. Kassi could be used for all types of exchange: negotiated, reciprocal, and generalized. This ambiguity led to some confusion and caution as well as speculation that others' inactivity on the site might be due to them not knowing what to offer or how to reciprocate. Early on, our research indicated that while most users held favorable attitudes towards the system, there were many reasons for not using the service (Suhonen et al., 2010). In addition to not living close enough for participation to be practical or just not being sufficiently interested in the service to take part, community members mentioned the difficulty of figuring out what items and favors to list, feelings of having nothing to offer, and uncertainty about the service and the kinds of action that would be appropriate and expected on the site.

Later on, we wanted to understand how Kassi was used for non-monetary exchange in particular, including gifting, lending, and borrowing (Lampinen et al., 2013). At the time, these constituted only a fraction (about 16%) of the listings on Kassi, while more typical activities included selling used textbooks and searching for housing. To understand experiences of non-monetary exchange—an activity we found particularly interesting because of the social dynamics it entails—we conducted in-depth interviews with individuals who had used the system. Rather than the concerns about freeriding we had anticipated, our participants shared accounts of the discomfort of feeling indebted to someone and of their reluctance to be on the receiving end of the exchange: First, participants expressed an aversion to indebtedness and talked about the importance of (perceived) fairness. Second, they frequently brought up their eagerness to provide something of value to others in the local community. They were reluctant to receive without contributing or at least knowing that they would get opportunities to contribute in the future. They also felt that others, too, should follow this guideline of giving and taking in commensurate ways. This resonates with prior findings about peer-to-peer exchange online: individuals tend to feel an obligation to return the benefits they receive from others, and they are psychologically and emotionally averse to over-benefiting from social interactions (Willer et al., 2012). Non-reciprocated actions can leave one with an uncomfortable sense of indebtedness—even if the original action or gift was unsolicited.

## 4.1.1   CONTRADICTORY FRAMINGS: AVERSION TO INDEBTEDNESS AND EAGERNESS TO CONTRIBUTE

Participants enjoyed making contributions to the community, but they did not necessarily expect others to feel the same way. Rather, they expressed concern about burdening or bothering others with their needs. These somewhat contradictory framings of one's own participation versus that of others are at the heart of why it is so easy to fail to appreciate the value that one provides as a beneficiary of others' contributions. Let us consider this tension in more detail.

An aversion to feeling indebted at the completion of an exchange was widely present in our interview material. Some participants explicitly stressed that they did not want to ask for something without being able to give something in return. They noted that indebtedness feels unpleasant and worrisome. One participant concluded her description of a good experience of receiving a favor via Kassi by bringing up that since she had yet to have an opportunity to return the favor to someone in the community, she was stuck with a debt of gratitude: "*I don't think it could have gone any better. But I have not gotten a chance to return the favor to anyone, so I still owe that favor.*" An appreciation for the norm of reciprocity was present also in the rest of the interviews, albeit in a less explicit form, in participants' expectations that neither of the exchange partners remains indebted. A striving for self-reliance was central. One participant expressed an extreme view of how one should live without being dependent on others: "*The way I see it people should survive on their own. I don't want to bother others in that way. I somehow avoid the sense of being indebted.*" Others were not as strictly against asking for help but they, too, thought it best to resort to others' goodwill only when in a serious need. The worry of burdening others was well illustrated by one participant's comparison: "*If you don't really need it, then it feels a little like being a parasite, that you bother others without a reason.*" While our interviews were specific to a particular, tight-knit student community embedded in the generally trusting and cooperation-oriented Finnish society, the insights from user responses and behaviors can apply to peer-to-peer exchange more broadly.

That agreeing to take on another person's offer—thus allowing them to contribute—might benefit the community on the whole (by fostering exchange activity and allowing others to feel safe in accepting offers or in requesting directly what they were missing) was not a part of our participants' expressed modes of thinking. Instead, in the initial process of making requests and responding to offers, participants expressed concern about being a burden or a nuisance. They did not want to ask for excessive efforts from others. One participant illustrated when he recalled the delighted surprise of noticing that the person who was lending him an electronic drill was so happy to help him use it: "*Well, I assumed that I would be more of a nuisance to that fellow. But on the contrary, he seemed really happy [in the situation].*" Yet, for a peer-to-peer exchange system to work, especially when generalized exchange is a part of its modes of operation, it is crucial that there be not only those willing to contribute but also those willing to accept contributions. The same has been noticed with timebanks: They can struggle with "getting the engine started" if members are reluctant to get more than they give. Sometimes they state explicitly that members are welcome to receive others' time before donating theirs so as to make it easier to get started. They may also communicate an acceptable range within which members' accounts should remain, making it clear that it is ok to go into red at times but also prompting members to use the hours they have accumulated.[3]

Less surprisingly, participants also indicated that they did not want to be cheated into bad or unfair deals. This is where we heard a sense of the fear of being taken advantage of that we had expected to be a central obstacle to participation. So, the participants were not taking part from a place of saint-like generosity—while they would have disapproved of others' freeriding, they were more preoccupied with ensuring that there would be no reason to think they themselves were taking advantage of others. Participants considered it better to give too much or to withdraw from participating altogether than to feel indebted to others. They thought it best to aim for "fair reciprocity." For instance, one participant who offered proofreading of English texts via Kassi explained that there were, of course, limits to her willingness to provide this service without some kind of bartering or compensation: "I think if it's a small thing, I could just do it for them but if they wanted me to proofread like a thesis, or really, something really big, then that should be more like some kind of trade or service." Overall, when it comes to the non-negotiated exchanges that our analysis focused on, our interviewees seemed to be more preoccupied with being fair-minded and avoiding indebtedness than worried about unfair treatment or being taken advantage of.

Our participants expressed an eagerness to contribute to the community. Those who had gotten the chance to offer something, expressed the most reward from actions that clearly contributed something of value to other community members. Being able to help out and contribute felt rewarding: "*It makes me feel good, when I lend things.—And then it makes me feel good, too, to be able to help someone else own fewer things. By lending what I have.*" Participants expressed getting a lot out of "helping others" (by responding to a request or offering something to others), especially when they felt that their efforts were valued and appreciated: "*I noticed that people are grateful that someone comes and helps them, that makes me feel good for sure.*" Being able to contribute to the local community

---

[3]  https://stadinaikapankki.wordpress.com/tietoja/stadin-aikapankin-abc-toimintaperiaatteet-ja-tovietiketti/ (read on June 4, 2021)

was central to rendering participation meaningful. Moreover, participants appreciated opportunities to "give (back)" whenever they received something from someone else. Recipients often tried to reciprocate either directly with another individual or by providing something of their own to the community. Participants indicated that they would sometimes post an offer on the site after they received something from others, especially if their original offer for direct reciprocation had been rejected. These issues are precisely why *accepting help* can, somewhat counterintuitively, be such an important contribution to exchange arrangements that rely on reciprocity and communal ties.

## 4.1.2    ALLEVIATING UNEASY FEELINGS OF INDEBTEDNESS

Given that the Kassi system neither provided a clear expectation of direct vs indirect reciprocity nor technical functionality that would have encouraged tackling the question online, potential compensation was often negotiated face-to-face at the end of the exchange process. When it comes to providing favors, donating goods, or lending items, direct compensation is not always appropriate or even possible. Our study revealed several user behaviors that alleviated uneasy feelings associated with indebtedness or created a situation where personal obligation was significantly lessened: (1) offering small tokens of appreciation to exchange partners, (2) understanding and accepting the indirect nature of generalized exchange, (3) managing expectations by framing offers and requests carefully, (4) minimizing efforts needed in exchange processes, and (5) bartering and exchanging for a third party.

**Offering Small Tokens of Appreciation**. Sometimes participants navigated their way out of indebtedness by offering little tokens of appreciation for their exchange partners. These are best understood as symbolic gestures that eased feelings of obligation by converting a unilateral giving situation into one that approximates direct reciprocity. Importantly, these small tokens of appreciation were not supposed to be a direct compensation for the efforts and value provided by one's exchange partner. For example, one participant insisted on giving a small token of appreciation for the person who lent him a power tool, and explained in the interview how this had been important for feeling good about the exchange. Another participant explained how he always offered to reciprocate when someone gifted him books, although without a serious expectation that his offer would be accepted. It is worth noting that these gestures of appreciation were not important only for those who wanted to find a way to express their gratitude but also to those who offered help. As one participant explained, an unexpected, small acknowledgement could give a positive afterglow for the entire experience: *"I think that he was really grateful for that, you could see from how he left that box of chocolates for me. It made me feel really good, since he really didn't have to do that, as I had been the one to offer lending that item."* Discussions stemming from these small gestures liberated recipients from feelings of indebtedness and saved providers from walking away disappointed due to a seemingly ungrateful exchange partner.

**Understanding and Accepting the Indirect Nature of Generalized Exchange Over Time**. The idea of balancing out any debts of gratitude with the community over time, not directly with one's exchange partner, had been a part of the philosophy underlying Kassi since the service was first created. However, it was not communicated to users in any explicit way. For a few participants, the "pay it forward to the community" aspect of Kassi was what made participation in the system appealing but, overall, engaging in generalized exchange was not instinctive or self-evident. One participant explained the idea of generalized exchange in terms of being "*okay with the community*" over time—being able to give back to someone in the community could make it easier to accept the lack of direct reciprocity. However, it seemed to require some time to become familiar and comfortable with this mode of exchange. Sometimes community members taught one another, such as in the case of a participant whose feelings of indebtedness had lessened when an exchange partner (in this case, one of the developers of the service) had explained to her that direct reciprocation is not always necessary and that she could, instead, offer a favor to someone else later on.

**Managing Expectations of Reciprocity by Framing Offers and Requests Carefully**. As Kassi did not spell out how exactly users should manage and coordinate exchanges, people's expectations could differ. Three participants brought up that one way to smoothen exchange processes is to spell out expectations of reciprocity when making an offer or a request. A good example of the importance of framing listings clearly came from a participant who had used Kassi to join a carpool. While the compensation of the driver's efforts and investments were eventually (and successfully) negotiated face-to-face, the participant explained that the process would have felt even easier if the expectation of sharing fuel costs would have been spelled out explicitly in the listing online. Another participant made an offer to help people who were moving in or out of an apartment. He stated that he did not expect compensation but that he would not reject it either. Such a wording, perhaps unsurprisingly, had led others to reward him in a variety of ways. The participant felt comfortable about the situation since although no explicit agreement had been made, he figured there would be no need for negotiating the "right" level of compensation or reward. Having made his position clear, he was happy to leave it to his exchange partners to figure out if and how they wanted to thank him. The clarity of the initial online interactions was important for laying the ground for subsequent face-to-face interactions. When expectations about reciprocity were managed clearly, participants felt less awkward about getting involved.

**Minimizing the Efforts Needed in Exchange Processes**. Participants attempted to keep exchange processes as effortless as possible to reduce the burden on others, for instance by switching communication channels as the exchange process proceeded. On the other hand, participants also talked about being troubled when coordinating an exchange turned out to require more effort on their part than they had intended, especially when the person receiving an item or a favor was not actively working to complete the exchange. The sentiments of a participant who lent a backpack to another student nicely illustrate how, for her, kind deeds done for others implied that the recipient should shoulder the effort: "*Sophie returned it by bringing it back to our place. -- That, in my opinion, was a nice gesture since when I have lent something to someone it is nice if the borrower brings it back to me so that I don't need to bother (to pick up the item).*" When expectations of responsibility and account-ability were not met, participants felt burdened and expressed an overall sense of imbalance in the exchange. Participants worried not only about potential conflicts resulting from material damage, but also about the flow of the exchange process: indebtedness stems from both exchange outcomes and the efforts made during exchange processes.

**Bartering and Exchanging for a Third Party**. As an unexpected discovery, we identified examples where individuals turned to Kassi to solve someone else's problem: screening and/or posting listings with the intention of finding something that a friend, a significant other, or a housemate needs. For instance, one participant promised a friend to keep an eye out for skates. When she stumbled upon the right size of skates, she set up a meeting for the friend and the seller: "*And then, in the end, that friend of mine went to get the skates himself, as they were not even for me, I just said that I can keep an eye out for skates of his size and then there happened to be a pair [on offer].*" While these types of acts are almost certainly not intentional efforts to avoid indebtedness, they are an effective way to distance oneself from obligations of reciprocity. Also, those who get pulled into exchange experiences without their own initiative may experience less of a personal connection to receiving benefits—and therefore less indebtedness. This "search it forward" approach (where indi-viduals look for goods and services for others, rather than themselves) was rare in our material, but it could be a promising strategy for fostering beneficial activity within communities that practice generalized exchange.

## 4.2    BLENDING AND LAYERING DIFFERENT FORMS OF RECIPROCITY

Let us now turn to how reciprocity plays out in another form of peer-to-peer exchange: short-term accommodation via Couchsurfing and Airbnb. Given the Couchsurfing community's emphasis on non-monetary, generalized exchange, what is in it for the hosts? Why does anyone welcome strang-ers to their home like that? As for Airbnb, is there really anything to it but the money? We will first consider how different forms of reciprocity get blended and layered in hospitality exchange: Even after the agreed-upon payment has been taken care of via the Airbnb exchange platform, or when no direct payment is expected in Couchsurfing, there are acts of reciprocation that are needed to manage the exchange encounter interactionally, such as performing the roles of host and guest. Second, we will consider how Airbnb hosts' participation has to do with money but how, for them, the value of hospitality exchange is not solely about it.

## 4.2.1    DIFFERENT FORMS OF EXCHANGE BLEND WITH ONE ANOTHER

Longstanding lines of research in anthropology and sociology have worked to divide the world into commodity and gift economies, each with a separate logic for making value. Yet, as anthropologist Anna Lowenhaupt Tsing (2015, p. 122) points out in her ethnographic account of the Matsutake, where she explains how the mushroom are both gifts and commodities, "*the contrast between gift and commodity suffers when it hits the ground; most situations juxtapose and confuse these ideal types—or stretch outside them.*" The same seems to be true for network hospitality (and peer-to-peer exchange more broadly): Even when money may be the most obvious and effective means for evening out an exchange, it alone is often not enough for an exchange encounter to unfold in a satisfactory manner.

In Airbnb, direct negotiated exchange is the primary mode of engagement. Encounters between hosts and guests start with a clearly defined transaction: accommodation offered in exchange for an agreed-upon sum of money. Sometimes, there is not much more than that to the exchange—the host and the guest may never meet in person, the space rented may reveal little of the host as a person, and so on. Yet, despite concerns about money crowding out more sociable outcomes, our interviews with Airbnb hosts in Finland and in the U.S. indicate that the existence of a direct, negotiated exchange as the foundation for an economic encounter does not exclude the possibility for interpersonal interaction (Ikkala and Lampinen, 2015; Lampinen and Cheshire, 2016). Nor does it do away with the need for managing interpersonal aspects of the exchange: When hosts and guests do meet in person, be it only in the passing to hand over the keys or more extensively when both stay at the same property, what started as a clear-cut transaction can become more of a social encounter. Here, partly to ensure good reviews and partly beholden by common decorum, both hosts and guests are likely to put forth a polite and amicable presentation, acting out the roles of a good guest and a good host. Interestingly, even hosts who rarely met their guests face-to-face talked to us about being touched by the hand-written thank you notes that guests had left for them. These small acts served to make the exchange more enjoyable and intimate. They made the hosts feel valued and acknowledged, especially since no one had told the guests to make such gestures (unlike providing reviews, which is an activity explicitly prompted by the exchange platform). Similarly, hand-written welcome notes may add a personal touch that delights guests.

Gauging one another's expectations is key: what appears as too much interaction can be equally undesirable as what appears as too little interaction. (This is a theme that will be explored in more detail in Chapter 5.) Beyond interpersonal interactions that can range from passing moments of politeness to extensive conversations over shared meals, our interviews with on-site hosts in the San Francisco Bay Area (Lampinen and Cheshire, 2016) revealed a range of additional exchanges that followed from the initial, negotiated agreement made on the Airbnb platform. These included smaller monetary exchanges that took place off the platform, such as renting out bikes to guests or leaving beverages available at the short-term rental for guests to pick up in exchange for some cash. One host, Marissa, talked about offering to organize tickets to the opera for her guests as her annual subscription allowed her to get them for a discounted price. This constituted an additional act of hospitality that also helped to surface a shared interest in opera, making the social encounter more meaningful for both the host and her guests. It had, of course, the potential to benefit Marissa over time, too, as guests pleased with their stay would likely write praising reviews that would attract further guests. Other hosts in our studies gave examples of sharing meals or getting drinks together during the guests' stay. One interviewee shared her plans to go and stay with a former guest while travelling in Europe, while another explained how she had made a number of friends by hosting people who were in the process of relocating to San Francisco. We discovered instances of gift-giving, too. For example, Marissa explained that she would often come up with little treats for her guests: "*If it just comes around, we'll do something special.—A lot of guests bring us gifts. We often give gifts back.*" The provision of unilateral gifts—a common characteristic of non-monetary network hospitality—in the scope of Airbnb demonstrates how an initial negotiated monetary exchange may evolve and expand so as to resemble reciprocal, non-monetary practices. Here, much like in Tsing's remark above, gifts and commodities get blended, creating an encounter that defies simple, clear-cut categorization.

Similarly, while Couchsurfing officially involves no direct reciprocation among participants—as the debts of gratitude are supposed to even out on the level of the community over time in line with the logic of generalized reciprocity—this is not to say that hosts and guests do not reciprocate directly, too. Research on Couchsurfing consistently documents guests bringing small gifts to their hosts or offering a round of drinks or a meal for them (e.g., Bialski, 2012a)—very similarly as we saw with the small tokens of appreciation that Kassi users described. These are not intended to be economically equivalent with the value of the accommodation hosts provide (the expectation, after all, is for generalized reciprocity). Rather, they are a complementary, direct form of reciprocity that help make the exchange encounter pleasant. Moreover, intense social encounters themselves can serve as a form of direct reciprocation where guests are expected to "pay" for the hospitality by sharing stories and engaging in extended, in-depth conversations with the hosts (Bialski, 2012a; Molz, 2012). Such expectations were visible also in my interviews with Couchsurfing hosts who were disappointed and frustrated if guests treated them "like a hotel"—a place where guests pay for hospitality and, as customers, are free to come and go as they please. Hosts did not want to be paid for their hospitality but they did expect an interesting social encounter and some acknowledgement of their generosity.

## 4.2.2    THE VALUE OF AN EXCHANGE IS NOT JUST ABOUT MONEY

Beyond how an exchange takes place (*the mode of exchange*), there is the question of what is being exchanged. Let us now consider the different types of *value* that can be at play in hospitality exchange. As illustrated above, non-monetary exchange is not exchange without reciprocation, and while receiving payment may be the most obvious way to balance out an exchange, it is not the only one. Beyond straightforward payment and more symbolic acts of direct reciprocation such as expressions of gratitude, some of the value of hospitality exchange can lie in opportunities to gain a good reputation within the exchange system (as participants expect this to be valuable in the future) and to engage in social interactions, at least when participants feel empowered to do so on their own terms.

Receiving favorable reviews that future exchange partners can view on one's profile can be a more or less explicitly articulated—and often implicitly expected—form of reciprocation. On Couchsurfing and Airbnb alike, further participation becomes easier for both guests and hosts as they gain a good reputation in the form of online reviews. On Couchsurfing, hosts may be fairly open about the fact that they are welcoming guests so as to build up a good reputation before they head out for travels of their own. In other words, they offer accommodation in expectation of a time when they will want to be able to find places to stay via the platform. In this example of generalized reciprocity, guests' contributions to the hosts' online reputation serve as an intermediate step. Accumulating *reputational capital* in a similar way was common among the Airbnb hosts we interviewed in Finland (Ikkala and Lampinen, 2014, 2015). Instead of improving their odds at finding hosts' willing to welcome them in the future, though, hosts described raising the price of their rental as they accrued a larger number of positive reviews to their profile. In the interview study conducted in California (Lampinen and Cheshire, 2016), Adam—a remote host—explained how demand tends to increase over time, as a host accumulates a reputation on the site and there is proof that others have enjoyed staying at the particular place. He described how pricing can be adjusted in line with the number of requests: "*The accepted wisdom is you need to start low. Then, when you get reviews, you can start to jack up your price. I got to the point where I was receiving so many requests that it made sense for me to jack up the price.*" Another host explained that "*the price includes the safe feeling for the guests,*" meaning that as a host with a good reputation, renting from her was less risky and that the sense of safety came at a price. When it comes to monetizing network hospitality via Airbnb, a good reputation is worth a lot: it increases hosts' opportunities for earning and, in many cases, allows them to command a higher price if they so choose.

Reputation as a form of reciprocation becomes more complicated when we consider that network hospitality often takes place between more than just one guest and host. This became clear in my interviews with members of multi-person households that welcomed Couchsurfing guests: While some wrote reviews together, it was more common that there was one person in charge of the account that the household used for hosting. Typically, that person assumed responsibility of both managing requests and writing reviews (Lampinen, 2014). Of course, there is not necessarily anything wrong with dividing responsibilities and letting the most enthusiastic person take care of the bulk of coordinating hosting online (a practice we will revisit in the next chapter). Yet, this arrangement has implications for who gets to benefit from a reputation that has been accumulated to an online profile.

Opportunities for social interaction are a second example of the different kinds of value that can make participation worthwhile. Intense social encounters can serve as a form of direct reciprocation, especially in the context of Couchsurfing where guests are expected to "pay" for the hospitality by sharing stories and engaging in extended, in-depth conversations with the hosts (Bialski, 2012a; Molz, 2012). When hosts receive no direct monetary compensation for the hospitality they provide, guests can feel obliged to share stories and provide company so as not to appear rude. As was already mentioned, Couchsurfing hosts testified to disappointment when they had felt deprived of the attention they had expected from their guests (Lampinen, 2016). Interestingly, similar issues came up with Airbnb hosts (Ikkala and Lampinen, 2015; Lampinen and Cheshire, 2016), for whom money was an important but by far not the only reason to keep hosting. As an example, Shuli explained that she discontinued hosting via Airbnb after it turned out to be less enjoyable than she had expected. She highlighted that the monetary profits alone had not been enough to justify the lack of expected social benefit from hosting: "*I just didn't have as good a time as I thought I would. Like people just weren't as cool as I thought they would be, and so I stopped.*"

Finally, even where money is part of the equation, exchanges are often not simple matters of maximizing profits. Economic interests play an important role but money is also put in the service of social ends, such as selecting guests and managing their expectations. In an early study of Airbnb hosts in Finland, we found that some were willing to lower their asking price in order to increase the amount of inquiries they received and hence have more choice in picking guests they deemed trustworthy and/or otherwise appealing (Ikkala and Lampinen, 2015). In a later study in the US (Lampinen and Cheshire, 2016), some hosts discussed pricing their properties below their estimate of the market price in order to avoid guests who arrive with expectations of a five-star luxury hotel. For example, Emily intentionally offered below-market rates to promote the community and to attract youthful guests. Others chose to ask for a higher price with the intention of pricing out some types of guests and attracting others who they deemed less risky. Here's how Greg reasoned about pricing: "*If you got it really cheap, you might get like students or something.—If you got it a little higher, then you figure the people that are okay to pay that are maybe not gonna be as troublesome or something.*" Either way, the hosts were not just out to make as much money as possible but, rather, weighed in their own effort and comfort. They used money as a tool to manage expectations and foster social interactions in line with their preferences. The desire to control social situations that these practices illustrate is closely linked with closeness and intimacy (see Chapter 5) as well as questions of who gets to participate in peer-to-peer exchange and how easy it is for different people to do so (see Chapter 6).

## 4.3    CONCLUSION

Exchange experiences are always shaped by how reciprocation is handled. As the classics of social exchange theory teach us, reciprocity is the foundation of exchange (Emerson, 1972a, 1972b), and norms of obligation emerge to reinforce reciprocity. Without it, exchanges are experienced as unfair and relationships erode. However, along with positive benefits of solidarity from acts of reciprocity, there are also psychological and interpersonal challenges to reckon with. Be it a system built around transactions, direct barter, or generalized reciprocity, exchange always involves some type of reciprocation. As the examples in this chapter illustrate, the value that is being exchanged may be much more nuanced than just money in exchange for goods or services, ranging from reputational benefits to meaningful interpersonal interaction.

When it comes to navigating reciprocity and indebtedness, we are faced with tricky social dynamics: Fear of being a freeloader may be more pertinent than freeloading. While eager to contribute, people may be hesitant to accept similar offers from others when they themselves stand to benefit. The contradictory framings of one's own participation versus that of others are at the heart of why it is so easy to fail to appreciate the value that one can provide for a community as a beneficiary of others' contributions.

Since the dynamics of reciprocity can feel so counterintuitive, a challenge for design is to come up with systems that encourage all kinds of contributions, including both "giving" and "taking". Providing another community member an opportunity to be of help in one way or another can foster their willingness to take part. It can but make the exchange system more attractive and credible in the eyes of the community overall by adding to its liveliness. Being able to contribute by facilitating exchange that one is either not a part of—or at least is not the sole benefactor of—is another interesting example of how exchange arrangements might steer away from simplistic, clear-cut distinctions between giving and getting. Communicating and managing expectations is key for navigating reciprocity, and participants may need some help in learning new modes of reciprocation and getting comfortable with them. Moreover, we should be mindful that even when it comes to monetary exchange, clear-cut transactions get blended with other modes of reciprocation. Most exchange encounters defy straightforward categorization.

In order to design online social exchange systems in ways that are mindful of the challenges of reciprocity, then, it helps to understand the situationally varying social norms that guide exchange processes and related expectations regarding the rules of engagement. When we design for peer-to-peer exchange, we can introduce different modes of exchange purposefully to foster particular social qualities. We will return to the crucial challenge of finding ways to alleviate the discomfort of indebtedness without doing away with the norm of reciprocity in Chapter 7.

# CHAPTER 5

# Closeness and Intimacy

*"Opening up to the other person is always a gift;*
*the trust to communicate cannot await the other person's promise to reciprocate*
*or the conversation will never begin."*

— Iris Marion Young in *Asymmetrical Reciprocity*

Social encounters are always vulnerable, and especially so when they take place between those previously unacquainted. In seeking *intimacy* or *closeness*, we risk rejection. As Iris Marion Young (1997) puts it, opening up to the other person is always a gift—and a risk. Our gesture of opening up to the other person may not be welcomed, or our counterparts may be reluctant to reciprocate. On other occasions, in simply trying to attend to a practical matter, we get drawn into a much more involved social interaction than we expected. In some ways, this vulnerable state of affairs is how it has to be: the magic of a pleasant and exciting encounter with a stranger derives its value in part from having dared to take a risk that then led to a positive outcome.

Balancing intimacy requires work. As Zelizer (2005) has argued so powerfully in her scholarship on the encounters of intimacy and economy, economic activity intersects with interpersonal relations, and people invest a great deal of effort in defining and disciplining their relations in this regard. It takes energy to engage in a social encounter with a stranger, and even more so to sustain longer-term relationships. What is more—while stating it explicitly can feel subversive—even if we are attracted by the idea of closeness in peer-to-peer exchange, we are not necessarily prepared to make the effort and manage the vulnerabilities that accomplishing it in a fulfilling way would necessitate.

This chapter explores intimacy and closeness in peer-to-peer exchange, with a focus on network hospitality. Couchsurfing and the early Airbnb both focused on in-person encounters and often intense social interaction among hosts and guests. Meeting locals while traveling and sharing personal stories and communal meals with strangers was key to the narrative. Over the years, Couchsurfing has largely retained this ethos while Airbnb has transformed so that it now, more and more frequently, features clear-cut transactions where hosts and guests meet face-to-face only in the passing or, quite commonly, not at all. In considering the tensions at play in determining and achieving the right amount and the right types of interaction between exchange partners, this chapter draws on the framework of *interpersonal boundary regulation* (Altman, 1975, 1977; Altman and Gauvain, 1981). A brief introduction to the framework can be found in Sidebox 5.1.

The chapter consists of three empirical examples. First, I describe how those engaging in hosting via Couchsurfing negotiate the boundaries of and within their home together with other members of their household, coming to agreement about what can be opened up for guests and when.[4] Second, I discuss sociability between hosts and guests in Couchsurfing and Airbnb, making the case that the presence of a monetary transaction at the root of a hospitality exchange does not rule out sociable interactions. Rather, it can facilitate further social exchange.[5] Third, I consider the intimacy of homes and possessions. While the other examples in the chapter focus on how closeness and intimacy are achieved and regulated in the course of face-to-face interactions, here, I convey how a meaningful connection among exchange partners does not always require meeting in person.

**Sidebox 5.1: Interpersonal boundary regulation**

Social psychologist Irwin Altman (1975) defines *interpersonal boundary regulation* as consisting of the efforts needed for people to achieve contextually desirable degrees of social interaction and to build and sustain their relations with others and with the self. Over the decades following Altman's work, communication scholar Sandra Petronio (2002) has built on it to develop a theory of *communication privacy management* (CPM). This theory focuses on the management of disclosures of private information with the help of privacy rules, emphasizing its dialectical and cooperative nature.

Interpersonal boundary regulation is a dynamic process that people engage in to pace and regulate social interaction. The desire for social interaction and withdrawal from it fluctuate over time and with circumstances: There are times when a person or a group may be receptive and welcoming to outside inputs. In other moments, the same person or group will close off contact with the outside environment or at least wishes to do so. Boundary regulation involves both restricting access to interaction and seeking interaction to achieve the contextually desired degree of social interaction. Social relationships are characterized by this dialectic interplay of accessibility and inaccessibility wherein each is "anticipated and sought on a cyclical basis" (Altman and Gauvain, 1981, p. 314).

---

[4]   This section draws on research previously published in Lampinen (2014, 2016).

[5]   This section draws on research previously published in Ikkala and Lampinen (2014, 2015) and Lampinen and Cheshire (2016).

There is an optimal degree of access of the self to others at any given time—and it is unsatisfactory to deviate from this optimum in either direction, to what feels like too much or too little interaction. Interpersonal boundary regulation, then, is not solely a matter of restricting access to interaction. It is also about inviting interaction, conditionally and contextually, to achieve valued outcomes such as sharing thoughts and experiences with others. When boundary regulation efforts are successful, people feel neither isolated nor crowded. Beyond regulating moment-by-moment access to social interaction, people regulate boundaries also to build and sustain the relations they have with others and with themselves.

Regulating interpersonal boundaries takes effort: Individuals and groups use a range of behavioral, cultural, and environmental mechanisms to achieve a degree of interaction that matches their temporally fluctuating desires. Christena Nippert-Eng (2010) argues that the collection of rich and nuanced activities that people use to regulate access to, for instance, their space, time, activities, possessions, bodies, and sense of self are as endless as are the specific challenges that these activities are deployed to address.

When successful, interpersonal boundary regulation allows us to come to terms with who we are and how we relate with one another as we navigate everyday interactions. Regardless of the efforts that people make, conflict, confusion, and clashes in expectations—that is, boundary turbulence (Petronio, 2002)—occasionally take place. When there is boundary turbulence, people take corrective action to restore appropriate boundaries and also to integrate new information into the rule system so that coordination might function more smoothly in the future.

## 5.1    NEGOTIATING BOUNDARIES OF AND WITHIN HOMES, ONLINE AND OFFLINE

Inviting or not inviting someone to enter a home is a clear indicator of the occupants' desire for more or less social interaction (Altman and Gauvain, 1981). Such desires may be variable within a multi-person household. Early research on Couchsurfing emphasized the dynamics of host–guest relationships, with descriptions of how people negotiate access to personalized spaces and adopt roles that help create both new boundaries of how to act and new forms of familiarity between participants (Bialski, 2012a, 2012b; Buchberger, 2012; Zuev, 2012). Yet, several scholars have noted that encounters often do not take place between just one host and one guest (Bialski, 2012b; Buchberger, 2012): Many people share their homes with others who may get involved in hosting more or less voluntarily. The Couchsurfing website allows community members to find and come into contact with new people, but the resulting face-to-face encounters and the effort involved in making them pleasant may not be equally welcomed by everyone in a household. Introducing guests to domestic spaces "can cause unease to those who normally have a lot of control over that space" (Bialski, 2012a, p. 76), such as household members who have not been alerted to a guest's arrival or who are unaware of the context or conditions of a visit. With that as a starting point, let us consider how those engaging in hosting via Couchsurfing negotiate the boundaries of and within their home together with other members of their household. The account here builds on an interview study of how multi-person households, including both self-defined domestic partnerships and sets of loosely connected housemates, regulate access to their domestic sphere as they offer to host couchsurfers (Lampinen, 2014, 2016).

### 5.1.1   WELCOMING STRANGERS

Deciding to begin hosting couchsurfers represents a significant transition point in the life of a household. Hosting via Couchsurfing is a proactive step toward inviting more interaction to the household, albeit one typically taken cautiously to prevent being overwhelmed. As household members negotiate over hosting and prepare to welcome strangers (who have been deemed trustworthy based on information provided in an online profile and messages exchanged via a networked system), the necessity of agreeing on privacy rules regarding domestic space and interaction becomes—for a moment—unusually visible (Lampinen, 2016). This is interesting, as most of the time, such rules remain implicit. They are mostly a matter of mutual accommodation, not the outcome of explicit, formal processes of negotiation and agreement.

When household members have come into agreement to become hosts, many particular choices follow as they receive requests and negotiate whether to accept them. This can entail negotiating mismatched wishes among household members. After all, even when only some household members are eager to host, the activity affects everyone. Among the hosts I interviewed, when household members disagreed over whether to accept a particular CouchRequest, the idea was typically dropped. For example, Carl, a 24-year-old man living with two housemates, stressed that everyone should agree on hosting. To describe how each member has a veto to refuse hosting, he described a scenario in which a housemate is preparing for an exam and needs the house to be empty of distractions: "*We have to respect. We can't force him to have a couchsurfer at the house.*" Sometimes initial disagreement led to more delicate negotiations, such as when Jenna had persuaded her partner into welcoming couchsurfers from her country of origin, pushing the negotiation slightly by emphasizing the visit's importance for her and its presumed effortlessness. While there is no guarantee that rules would always be established in a fair and equal manner, at least according to their own accounts, participants did not want to insist or impose. Jenna, too, said that she would not invite couchsurfers without her partner's approval or risk getting into a fight about hosting. Since consensus was at a premium, those with the least desire to interact with guests held the power to limit whether and when to host. When compromises over hosting were needed, household members considered too little external interaction more acceptable than too much, and made decisions accordingly. As a rule, relationships within the household were given higher priority than the household's (potential) connections with visitors.

Couchsurfing profiles allow hosts to indicate how likely they are to agree to host. Several households had used switching between "*yes*" and "*maybe*" as a way to match the number of requests they received with the amount of hosting they desired to undertake at different times. As an example of this temporal fluctuation, Kevin explained how his household would move between agreeing and refusing to host: "*It's . . . kind of cyclical, comes in waves. We do it for a little while, get sick of it, and take a break from it, and do it again, take a break from it.*" Hosts' responses to requests varied over time partly because participants viewed hosting as more than just offering a place to stay. The perceived requirement for interaction with guests led many to refuse hosting unless all household members could make sufficient time for the visitors. Once hosts had agreed to accommodate someone, they felt obliged to make time for the guests and accept occasional discomforts, including a sense of unease, exhaustion, or even violation due to what felt like too much interaction. Various issues—for instance, hosting too many guests at a time or having guests stay for too long—could result in feeling overwhelmed. Even when everything went well with individual visits, hosts mentioned that hosting what felt like too many couchsurfers back-to-back or within a short time period lessened the joy of hosting and made them less willing to accept requests. Varying levels of participation over time made it easier for household members to avoid experiencing hosting as a burden.

## 5.1.2    COORDINATION AND COOPERATION AMONG HOUSEHOLD MEMBERS

Successful privacy management requires coordination and cooperation. Household members need to negotiate not only over what is made accessible but also who communicates these boundaries to visitors. Hosting challenges multi-person households to both regulate their collective exterior boundaries and attend internally to each member's personal boundaries. Some tactics for addressing these challenges involve delegating hosting responsibilities to more enthusiastic household members and taking turns in shouldering hosting responsibilities.

Although household members may share responsibilities over hosting, it is also possible for individuals to delegate particular privacy management tasks to others. Most participating households had one individual in charge of the household's account on Couchsurfing. At the time of the study, in setting up a profile—even one that was explicitly about several people—Couchsurfing allowed for inserting only one email address to which the system forwarded all messages sent to the profile owner(s). The system's affordance for forwarding messages to just one address reinforced the tendency for an individual to become a gatekeeper to the household's shared account. Delegating responsibility to the most enthusiastic individual allowed those who desired less interaction with guests to participate more passively. Some, like Kate and Jeff, wanted to manage hosting on a more equal footing, stressing the importance of discussing requests: "*We definitely always look at the request and talk about it together, before one of us would respond.*" Most households settled for a balance between complete delegation and full cooperation. Often the person who received messages forwarded them to others or brought them up in face-to-face conversations. Some shared everything diligently, while others selected only the most promising requests for joint consideration. Christina curated carefully the requests she brought into discussion with her husband John. Making hosting as meaningful and effortless as possible for him was her strategy for being able to continue hosting despite John's reluctance. Beyond the coordination of online communications prior to visits, household members could delegate responsibility of handling problems during visits to the primary host (if one was identifiable). Christina, who was comfortable with being upfront with visitors, sometimes agreed to express John's wishes on his behalf, bearing responsibility of regulating the availability of their home: "*I have a sense that we've had guests who sort of hung around more than John wanted—So what tends to happen in those situations is John comes to me and sort of grumbles like, 'He's still downstairs.'—I'll say, 'Okay would you like me to ask him to please get going so we have the house for the day?'*"

An individual can be put in charge of negotiating access to the household via Couchsurfing and handling conflicts with visitors, but during visits, responsibility over privacy management cannot always be fully delegated. Once hosting proceeded from online negotiations to face-to-face interaction, privacy management became a more cooperative effort, sometimes involving the practice of turn taking. The presence of multiple hosts relieves the pressure to interact with guests that each individual within the household experiences. Since multiple hosts can take turns, individuals in multi-person households can retreat from interaction more politely and comfortably, be it for a need to be left alone or to handle other commitments. In this way, taking turns in spending time with the guests allowed groups to take care of their individual members' needs cooperatively without the guilt of neglecting guests.

## 5.1.3  PHYSICAL AND TEMPORAL STRUCTURES IN PRIVACY MANAGEMENT

Negotiations over access to domestic spaces range beyond opening the front door to questions over who spends time with visitors, when, and in what spaces. Privacy management efforts that hosts undertake online make balancing interaction within the home easier, because many issues have already been settled by the time visitors arrive. During face-to-face encounters, spatial and temporal boundaries are leveraged to support privacy management. For instance, hosts relied on characteristics of the home to arrange opportunities for discrete conversations among household members.

Domestic space plays an important role in making hosts feel ready and willing to take on the challenges of hosting. The particulars differed, but some separateness was the baseline for what, in the interviewees' minds, constituted sufficient space for hosting. Most participating households either had an extra bedroom or the hosts had a bedroom separate from the space available for visitors. Mike explained how he always described the spatial arrangements to guests beforehand, ensuring that they would arrive with realistic expectations: "*I always tell people that you will have our living room all by yourselves but it has no door. Although me and Daniela have our bedroom.*" His partner Daniela added: "*Which does have a door, thank God.*" She considered it important to keep some spaces and times within the home inaccessible to visitors, presumably to grant the hosts the opportunity to withdraw from interacting with the guests and to maintain intimacy among household members. Participants' self-imposed requirement of providing sufficient space serves the comfort of both the guests and the hosts. Separate spaces allow drawing clear boundaries regarding which spaces guests may use.

Kevin and his housemates were comfortable foregoing explicit negotiation over particular visits. They were congenial about inviting visitors to their shared living room. Kevin informed everyone about upcoming visits, explaining that a separate conversation about whether to host was typically unnecessary because all kinds of guests were a common occurrence in the household and having couchsurfers was just another addition to the social life of the house. Housemates' rooms, however, remained, by default, their private territory. Matt and David's comfort in delegating negotiations to Kevin seemed to rely on knowing that they could always retreat to their rooms if they wanted to be alone. This is an example of how in communal households, the rooms of each housemate tended to be off-limits for guests (and even for other household members) both day and night, and as a result, negotiations regarding hosting focused on whether and when shared spaces were made available for visitors. It is worth noting, though, that while some domestic spaces remained by default off-limits to guests, these spatial boundaries were somewhat fluid: Many hosts saw no reason for the guests to enter certain areas in the home, but guests could be given permission to use them if they, for instance, needed to make a phone call in private.

Temporal structures were interwoven with these spatial arrangements. As Lynch, Di Domenico, and Sweeney (2007) depict in their account of cultural homestays in commercial homes, the accessibility of different domestic spaces is not only a matter of distinguishing between public spaces used by both inhabitants and guests and other spaces that are used exclusively by the long-term occupants. Rather, spatial boundaries are wrapped together with time—ownership over different spaces can shift during the course of the day. For example, at times, hosts waited to have private discussions during the day when guests were out, or at night, when bedroom doors were closed. In addition to sleeping space arrangements in which the living room is a shared space for socializing during the day and visitors' territory by night, guests and hosts negotiated turns in using kitchens and bathrooms. Although hosts welcomed guests to use their kitchen, taking up this offer sometimes introduced coordination challenges and interruptions to household routines. Similarly, while sociable encounters were a key reason to host, Couchsurfers' eagerness to interact sometimes became problematic late in the evenings as the hosts wanted to retreat to get a good night's sleep before heading to work the next morning. Guests and hosts differ, among other things, in that guests tend to have leisure time while hosts are not removed from the rhythm of work and everyday obligations (Zuev, 2012). Accordingly, the hosts I interviewed made efforts to manage privacy in spatially and temporally nuanced ways, in line with their wish to have guests willingly open up to them while retaining control over when such disclosures take place.

Finally, large parts of what makes network hospitality a socially compelling activity happen beyond the reach of the Couchsurfing interface. Yet, over time, efforts to manage boundaries during face-to-face interactions are reflected in and geared to complement action that is taken online. Accumulating hosting experience helped households and their individual members to figure out how to regulate their collective and personal privacy boundaries more effectively. It was typical for the hosts to act upon perceived privacy turbulence in a twofold fashion: First, they tried to be tolerant during particular visits. Second, they made efforts to prevent similar discomforts in the future by updating their profile or by resolving to handle requests differently.

Online profiles were used to convey expectations and restrictions, thus drawing a baseline for negotiating individual visits. Hosting experiences, for their part, informed how profiles should be updated to facilitate future negotiations. Profiles were not updated frequently, but when they were, changes were often prompted by privacy turbulence, such as an overwhelming hosting experience. For instance, hosting four college students at once had led Jenna and Simon to decrease the number of visitors they proposed to welcome at any one time (a piece of information visible on their Couchsurfing profile): *"When we had the four kids, like the four college people, and it was a mess, [we] said 'okay, no more four people at the same time. Three's the max.'—Just like, we're both tired, and we said, 'Okay, four is too much.'"*

Learning from uncomfortable experiences allowed participants to pursue hosting as smoothly as possible. Discussions after visits were an important site of renegotiating hosting among household members. These moments of reflection allowed the household members to express concerns, determine whether and how to continue hosting, and figure out how to communicate such preferences in their profile on the Couchsurfing website. Practicing network hospitality cooperatively can provide sought-after social encounters, but realizing this objective requires efforts both online, where networked technologies are used to manage privacy in a preventive and corrective fashion, and offline, where boundaries are managed and negotiated in person during and between visits.

## 5.2 THE ROLE OF MONEY—OR ITS ABSENCE—IN SOCIABILITY AMONG HOSTS AND GUESTS

This section grapples with the role that monetary exchange—or its absence—plays for sociability in host–guest relationships. Scholarship on Couchsurfing (Bialski, 2012a; Molz, 2014; Lampinen,

2014) has emphasized the value of intense, sociable encounters for both hosts and guests, while our early research on Airbnb (Ikkala and Lampinen, 2015; Lampinen and Cheshire, 2016) indicates that the initial monetary exchange between hosts and guests does not rule out sociable interactions. It is a legitimate concern that encouraging hosts to monetize the housing assets available to them (like Airbnb does) can create an ideological tension with non-monetary hospitality exchange systems (like Couchsurfing) that are specifically targeted to promote prosocial behavior and respectful cultural exchange through interpersonal connections.[6] However, it seems that the presence of money in peer-to-peer exchange can, at least in some cases, even support sociable interaction (Ikkala and Lampinen, 2015; Lampinen and Cheshire, 2016) by alleviating perceived social obligations (such as being available for intense host–guest interaction).

### 5.2.1 ECONOMIC CONSIDERATIONS LURK UNDER THE SURFACE OF NON-MONETARY EXCHANGE

Before we turn to Airbnb, let us briefly consider how network hospitality via Couchsurfing, while non-monetary, is not free of economic considerations. First, of course, hoping to find accommodation seemingly for free can be an important reason for guests to turn to Couchsurfing. Second, as we saw in Chapter 4, Couchsurfing hosts repeatedly listed guests who were "*only using us as a hotel*" as a source of disappointment and frustration. It was hurtful for them to have opened up their homes, only to find out that the guests seemed only interested in free accommodation. Hosts' sentiments of being deprived of attention they had expected echo the point that boundary regulation may fail toward not just too much but also *too little* interaction. For example, Laura and Marco, a couple in their early 30s had felt ignored and taken advantage of on their first attempt at hosting. While they considered giving hosting another chance, Laura was apprehensive: "*I think definitely it would be helpful if someone who comes to my house would be open and willing to meet me ... because our feeling was that we were just used to give someone space.*" Bob shared a similar experience that had not met his expectation of an interesting social encounter: "*She didn't interact a lot with us... We had a pretty bad feeling about her, because she was just sleeping and going to a conference... For me, Couchsurfing is... more than just not being in your hotel; you have to be ready to share things, you have to spend time with the people that are hosting you.*" On the flipside, stories of guests overstaying their welcome or taking up more time and space than the hosts had expected were not absent from Couchsurfing hosts' accounts, either. Initially welcome guests could start to feel like a burden, if they asked for more than the host deemed reasonable. Finding the right level of interaction and engagement is not always easy. It takes willingness and skill from both hosts and guests to achieve a pleasant, sociable encounter. Even when money is not changing hands, interactions with strangers are never free of expectations. The ban on using money to reciprocate frames interactions between couchsurfers and their hosts, setting up expectations of availability to sociable, even intense, interaction. When such

[6]   http://about.couchsurfing.com/about/about-us/ (read on June 4, 2021)

expectations are not met, we can observe a glimmer of the economic considerations that lurk under the surface: hosts can quickly lose their interest in offering free accommodation if their generosity is not met with gratitude or if their guests fail to show interest in interacting with them.

## 5.2.2   MONETARY EXCHANGE DOES NOT RULE OUT SOCIABLE INTERACTIONS

Airbnb adds an explicit financial exchange to the online–offline sharing context that was pioneered by services like Couchsurfing. The underlying form of exchange is important since it influences decisions to engage in social exchange in the presence of risk and uncertainty (Cheshire et al., 2010), such as welcoming a stranger to one's home. In our interviews with Airbnb hosts in California in 2014, we found that the core monetary exchange at the root of host–guest relationships in Airbnb helped hosts in two ways. First, by using the online system as a broker for the monetary transaction, hosts could comfortably manage expectations on their terms. Second, hosts described how the core monetary exchange facilitated additional social exchange—it turned strangers into less risky exchange partners.

Since Airbnb acts as a third party that confirms the transaction between the host and the guest—that is, it creates an assurance structure (Molm et al., 2009)—the transaction itself is much less risky and less uncertain compared to non-binding negotiations (Cook and Cheshire, 2013; Molm et al., 2009). In creating an assurance structure, Airbnb facilitates the core financial transaction so that both host and guest know that payment has completed successfully without ever having to talk about or directly exchange money. Payments do not need to be made face-to-face, they are handled via the platform which maintains a centralized data repository documenting details of all exchanges. When Airbnb guests arrive, their stay is already fully paid. This means that the host need not worry about getting the agreed upon compensation—a common concern, for instance, when it comes to selling things via Craigslist or Facebook groups for peer-to-peer sales (Moser et al., 2017). Hiding away the monetary exchange can serve to enable a performance of friendliness that would be difficult to accomplish if the host and guest needed to address money explicitly: Maria who had hosted via both Couchsurfing and Airbnb highlighted these issues in depicting her experiences of interaction with Airbnb guests: "*[I]t could be so awkward. It's really not. Because everything is, the transaction is handled behind the scenes. When they show up, they're fully paid, and you don't have to worry about that.—I think that that helps the social interaction to not be [as] weird as it could be.*" By foregoing the in-person payment ritual, the interaction can feel less awkward.

For most interviewees, the core exchange reduced risks and uncertainties, making it easier for some to become a host and enjoy valued social interaction and other ancillary benefits of network hospitality (Lampinen and Cheshire, 2016). The potential distance that money creates between actors, then, does not exclude the possibility of meaningful, sociable interaction between individuals. On the contrary, the presence of money and the existence of a clear price for the network hospitality that is being offered may provide conditions in which sociable interaction can flourish—even more easily than it might in non-monetary network hospitality, wherein concerns over indebtedness and reciprocity may complicate interpersonal connections. Bialski (2012a) has expressed a similar idea in relation to hitchhiking websites via which passengers pay for the ride. She reflects on how the presence of money can change the social dynamics of the situation: "*Perhaps the sociality that emerges despite the explicit nature of the reciprocity deems the conversation less instrumental, more voluntary, than the conversation and interaction in some cases during the implicit reciprocity between Couchsurfers.*" Sociability, similar to that observed in Couchsurfing, can persist in contexts structured by negotiated, monetary exchange. In some cases, the presence of money may even contribute to the flourishing of voluntary, enjoyable interaction that entails lesser sense of obligation and that, in this, approaches Simmel's ideal of pure sociability (Simmel, 1903/1950) as a valuable social form (Ikkala and Lampinen, 2015).

In networked hospitality exchange, monetary transactions frame the exchange relation in a way that can contribute to the fluency of the exchange process. Several of the hosts we interviewed in California highlighted the value of the flexibility in choosing how to host, including considerations regarding length of stay, number of guests at a time, space provided, as well as the amount of interaction with guests. By negotiating the terms of the financial exchange, hosts and guests are able to regulate the amount of social interaction with one another in line with their preferences. While potential earnings were important for hosts in both Finland and the U.S. (Ikkala and Lampinen, 2015; Lampinen and Cheshire, 2016), the perceived or expected social benefits mattered to them, too. (Note, however, that I am not arguing this would be the case for all Airbnb hosts.) For instance, Cynthia described things she and her guests might do together: "*On occasion, if I like someone and I have free time, I'll take 'em somewhere like to the beach or just give 'em a drive around. And with some people, we'll eat dinner together sometimes or play cards or go to the movies.*" Social interaction with guests was a significant motivation for some Airbnb hosts. Simultaneously, at least at times, it was experienced as a burden by others.

Sometimes participants' needs do not align neatly: what is too much or too intimate for one may be too little for the other. When asked about difficult Airbnb experiences, Greg described a time when he as a guest had been pulled into conversations that were much more intense and personal than he would have preferred: "*It wasn't really that bad, but it was weird because basically, what happened was this guy had gotten divorced, and his daughter had died or something. And he tells me this because I'm staying in the dead daughter's room, which he told me, which is awkward because I'm like, 'Oh. Your daughter just died.' And he needs his wife—I don't know. I think she left him or something, and so, yeah. Just this very sad story. Then I feel guilty. I feel like I'm therapy for him. I think that's how it was for him.—And then that feels awkward 'cause I don't—I don't wanna be mean, but I'm just like, 'I really just wanted to sleep here'. I don't wanna—I don't wanna—I don't wanna have all these conversations, especially this thing. Now I'm sleeping in your dead daughter's bed. It's really weird.*" Even as a clear price tag can go a long way to clarify the scope of an exchange, it does not do away with the challenges related to participants' contextually different desires for social interaction. Wrestling with considerations regarding closeness was common in interviews with Airbnb hosts, too, much like with Couchsurfing hosts.

Motivations for participation vary both between hosts and over time. To illustrate Airbnb hosting that is clearly more instrumental and less sociable than welcoming couchsurfers, let's consider Adam who hosted via both Airbnb (remotely) and Couchsurfing (on-site). He explained that the two served different purposes for him: "*I only host Couchsurfing occasionally. And I usually do Airbnb when I need to make money. So, I, most of the time, I'm too busy for either.*" Adam emphasized that social interaction was the key feature of, and reason for, hosting couchsurfers: "*[T]he difference I see is, when I have a Couchsurfing guest, I don't spend a whole lot of time cleaning my apartment beforehand. I view it more as 'I'm going to have this person sleep [on] my futon. I'm going to sleep in the bed.—We're gonna go out for a drink or dinner. We're gonna get to know each other.*'"

In some Airbnb hosts' accounts, guests would sometimes behave as entitled customers who had little interest in doing their part of making the social interaction pleasant, or even merely functional. Contrasting Airbnb to Couchsurfing, Emily, who, like Adam, had experience of hosting guests via both services, highlighted that the monetary nature of exchange means that Airbnb guests may have higher expectations and that they are more willing to ask for things if they feel that the expectations are not met: "*I felt like the one difference, besides the money, was that people on Airbnb definitely expected things more cuz they're paying. So they would, not demand things but ask politely for things and expect certain things. Then with Couchsurfing they were so grateful and maybe made me dinner.*" As Airbnb guests were more prone to act as customers compared to couchsurfers, Emily explained that she chose to keep rates low partly in an effort to manage expectations and fend off overly demanding guests. This choice also created opportunities for sociable encounters with visitors from across the world—something that made up for Emily's own limited travel opportunities at the time of the interview. While there is much variation between hosts—and while the culture of Airbnb has shifted over time —at least some Airbnb hosts are driven to monetize network hospitality not just because of the money they can make but also because they find the sociality of the practice pleasurable.

When it comes to ongoing debates over the nature and potential of the sharing economy, the presence of money has emerged as a central point of contention. On a higher structural level, there certainly is much to reconcile between the ethos of cosmopolitan sharing and the logics on which venture-backed exchange platforms operate. That said, when we look at interpersonal interactions between hosts and guests—importantly, with a focus on the experiences of individuals who monetize network hospitality on a relatively small financial scale—what we see is that sociability between hosts and guests is not just a misplaced fantasy and that there need not exist a contradiction between monetary and social motives for participation. Binding negotiated exchange as an initial form of interaction between hosts and guests reduces uncertainty for hosts. It makes it easier for them to manage encounters and facilitates further social exchange and interaction with guests, sometimes of a variety normally reserved for friends and family. While the presence of money can even be helpful for the sociable interaction and sense of connection many seek in engaging with network hospitality, this does not alleviate the need to think critically about the interpersonal implications that money may have in this context and, as has become evident over the years, the effects that monetizing network hospitality may have on neighborhoods, cities, and societies at large.

## 5.3    ASYNCHRONOUS INTIMACY

The core binding negotiated transaction that Airbnb facilitates between hosts and guests often served as a gateway to further social exchanges and unexpected intrinsic motivations to continue hosting: On-site hosts expressed how important it was to meet new people. Both on-site and remote hosts appreciated not only the money they could make by hosting but also the opportunities to surprise or delight guests, and to feel like they were "giving something back" to others. While this chapter has so far focused primarily on how closeness is achieved and regulated in the course of the face-to-face interactions that network hospitality can entail (and how online activities complement such efforts), this section invites us to briefly consider the intimacy of homes, possessions, and local knowledge.

In both Finland and in the U.S., the Airbnb hosts who practiced remote hospitality and, accordingly, had little in-person interaction with their guests, sometimes described experiences of a sense of closeness—asynchronous intimacy—in letting guests use the private space of their home. Opening up the home for strangers, preparing it for them, and striving to facilitate a comfortable and satisfying visit felt socially significant and even intimate, also when it involved little (or no) face-to-face interaction. For instance, Maria explained that her guests had been very appreciative of all forms of kindness that exceeded the negotiated terms of the exchange, such as tips about where to go: "*[regarding] Airbnb people, my experience has been that because they are paying for it, --they value it more, and so they are often quite effusive about how grateful they are, about your maps, or your lists of the coolest five bars in the neighborhood.*" Guests' expressions of gratitude made hosting more gratifying, even as she had scarce face-to-face interactions with them.

Receiving the occasional hand-written note from guests who acknowledged these efforts felt rewarding and contributed meaningfully to a sense of connectedness. Several of the hosts we interviewed described gratification stemming from being recognized as a competent host and succeeding in surprising one's guests positively. Adam's depiction of hosting as gratifying work captures these sentiments poignantly: "*There's something very nice about when you show a guest in, and, not to say that this happens all the time, but their eyes light up because I've worked so hard on making this place spotless.—And it sounds kind of silly to say that preparing a studio could be this work of pride, but it is.*"

For some, the experience of sharing something of their life extended beyond the walls of the home to sharing their city. Sharing one's local expertise was another commonly mentioned aspect of acting out the role of a good host. Jennifer described the enjoyment she found in giving recommendations to guests: *"I'm going to host our place on Airbnb for like other, you know people who don't wanna pay a ton, but want a cool experience. I, personally, really love giving recommendations on places."* While the remote hosts did not spend much (or any) face-to-face time with guests, most were happy to provide useful information, such as maps and tips on what to do. In experiences of asynchronous intimacy, offering tips about favorite restaurants and things to do locally were important ways to share something personal with the guests and give them a glimpse into one's life.

The research this chapter builds upon was not geared to capture guest perspectives, yet many of the hosts we interviewed shared first-hand experiences of using Airbnb as guests, too. Their accounts of these experiences point to a similar imagination being at play for guests who, for their part, may look for "authentic" experiences and value the opportunity to stay in a "local" home, even if they meet the hosts only in the passing (or not at all). As a personal experience to illustrate this point, I remember vividly staying in a single-family home in Alabama, U.S., where I never met the hosts face-to-face. My partner and I stayed a night surrounded by the hosts' possessions, including deeply personal items like wedding photos. What is more, the hosts' pet pig was staying in the backyard! While we were not asked to care for it, it felt like a trusting gesture on the hosts' part to leave their pet in the company of strangers, unattended.

From the guests' perspective, staying in a stranger's home while the host is not present can feel very intimate and leave lasting (and sometimes odd) memories of gaining a particular view into someone else's life. Of course, not all Airbnb stays where the host is not present have such qualities. Far from it, Airbnb enables a lot of faceless, distant transactions where it is glaringly obvious (and often expected) that the space rented is not anyone's actual residence. When it comes to the "authenticity" and experiences of "living like a local" that Airbnb markets and that guests may find appealing, large parts of the narrative is best thought of as a performance. Yet, hosts and guests alike can find value in exchanges that involve asynchronous intimacy. Face-to-face interaction is not the only possible source of a sense of intimacy in exchange processes, and it seems that in monetary hospitality exchange—even in its remote form where the host is not present during the guest's stay —there still exists a residue of traditional forms of hospitality exchange in which exchange of material and symbolic gifts play a role in establishing and consolidating social ties. While the amount and type of interaction comes up in moral assessments of whether particular exchange activities can be meaningfully characterized as part of a sharing economy, it seems like a mistake to position face-to-face as the implicit gold standard for assessing social interaction and experiences of closeness.

## 5.4    CONCLUSION

The interactions involved in peer-to-peer exchange—be it network hospitality or something else—are neither obvious nor without risk. They may feel vulnerable and effortful, and sometimes exchange partners' wishes clash. The presence of clear-cut monetary transactions may contribute to hosts' sense of control by making it easier for the exchange partners to adopt a shared definition of the exchange situation and accomplish desired sociability. This, in turn, is helpful in coordinating the entire exchange process. Face-to-face interaction does not feature in—and is not sought for—in all instances of peer-to-peer exchange. As such, when studying and designing for such exchanges, it is worth attending to the value of social distance in accomplishing desired types of sociality (Lampinen et al., 2017).

The possibility of better-connected local neighborhoods and meaningful social encounters among strangers was central to early enthusiasm about the sharing economy (Suhonen et al., 2010). So, too, was the notion of tourists and locals coming together for mutually enriching interactions (Molz, 2014). However, the success of the former efforts has been halting, and the authenticity of the latter under constant debate. Here, we can hear echoes of Zelizer's (2005) term *hostile worlds* which captures the basic premise that economic transactions and intimate relationships do not fit together and must be kept separate if the intimate is to retain its value and importance. I argue, though, that an approach akin to Zelizer's (2005) proposal of *connected* lives does more to serve our inquiries into how relationships in the sharing economy unfold, as it invites us to consider the relational work that goes into managing where different relationships fall on a continuum from the impersonal to the intimate. When it comes to platform-mediated peer-to-peer exchange (and network hospitality in particular), there are always these types of relational issues that the exchange partners, ultimately, have to negotiate on their own. That said, exchange platforms have a role to play in setting up expectations and norms, encouraging or discouraging particular types of behavior, and establishing the baseline for how much needs to be handled interpersonally.

While Couchsurfing and Airbnb are both geared toward helping hosts and guests in organizing short-term stays, they differ drastically in how these exchanges are negotiated. At a glance, one might conclude that Airbnb has simply been more successful in making it quick and easy for hosts and guests to match up for an exchange, especially given the increasing prevalence of the InstantBook feature that allows guests to book accommodation directly rather than having to first reach out to the host, introduce themselves, and explain why they wish to book this particular place. Yet, as Klein et al. (2017) document in their analysis of Couchsurfing and Airbnb dual-users, there are vastly diverging expectations between the two services. In a nutshell, compared to Couchsurfing, Airbnb appears to require higher quality services, places more emphasis on places over people, and shifts social power from hosts to guests. While Airbnb certainly seems to have outgrown Couchsurfing over the past years (Klein et al., 2017), considering the issue solely as a matter of efficiency and one platform being more successful than the other is insufficient (Lampinen and Brown, 2017). The difference here is not just a matter of Airbnb being more effective than Couchsurfing. The streamlined booking flows Airbnb offers can certainly be convenient for both hosts and guests (and they can help to combat discriminatory outcomes). This is in stark contrast to the uncertainty of finding accommodation via Couchsurfing and the effort it can take from couchsurfers to communicate with many enough hosts to find someone who agrees to host them in a suitable location at a suitable time.

The differences in the specific features Airbnb and Couchsurfing provide for connecting hosts and guests foster different social qualities in the hospitality exchanges that the two platforms facilitate. As Parigi and State (2014) have pointed out, technology can increase the ease of establishing interpersonal connections with strangers while, simultaneously, diminishing the bonding power of such experiences. Parigi and State originally depicted this process of disenchantment in the context of the rising popularity of Couchsurfing between 2003 and 2011. Here, I bring it up as an example of how service design that necessitates more back-and-forth messaging between hosts and guests to set up a stay can foster interpersonal outcomes and, in particular, trust between those involved. Platforms like Couchsurfing that are committed to promoting interpersonal connections and sociable encounters might choose to prioritize such outcomes, even at a cost to effectiveness and convenience. In some cases, the ease that automation can bring about in coordinating exchanges is desirable. In others, the choice might be made to promote the social qualities that more effortful and vulnerable interactions can bring about. Efficiency involves trade-offs, and so does a strict push for closeness among exchange partners.

While platforms shape and direct the activities they facilitate, this is not to undermine the agency of those involved in peer-to-peer exchange. Those who are looking to exchange on a marketplace differ from one another and they may also desire different things at different times. Some seek more personal encounters, while others—or the same participants at other times and in settings—may prefer clear-cut, socially distant transactions. We should be cautious not to assume, even if only implicitly, that closeness should (or could) always be a characteristic of "successful" peer-to-peer exchange. A more productive approach might be to ask whether participants want to foster closeness, and if so, with whom, in what form, and under what conditions. To foster desired social qualities, we need to understand participants' wishes and then, perhaps, nudge them to do the work that their preferred outcomes require, regardless of whether the aim is to uphold a sense of distance characteristic of impersonal transacting or to foster a more intimate connection akin to an encounter with a friend.

CHAPTER 6

# Participation and Inclusion

*"Participation is about power,
and no matter how 'open' a platform is, participation will reach a limit
circumscribing power and its distribution."*

— Chris Kelty in *From Participation to Power*

Participation is a term that gets used a lot, in vague and variable ways but typically with a positive normative value (Kelty, 2013; Vines et al., 2013). The idea of participatory culture (Jenkins, 2009), where individuals do not act only as consumers but also producers, is at the heart of most of the social computing systems that surround us today: barriers to contributing are meant to be low, and while not everyone will contribute, all should feel that they are free to do so and that their contributions will be welcomed. These same ideas permeate the domain of peer-to-peer exchange, with many researchers focused on how to attract people to join exchange communities and what might encourage them to say involved over time (e.g., Bellotti et al., 2015; Ganglbauer et al., 2014; Malmborg et al., 2015; Shih et al., 2015). Yet, as the quote from Chris Kelty implies, when it comes to participation, we should also reckon with questions of power: Who gets to be involved and how easily? Who is excluded? Who gets drawn in despite their wishes? How are the boundaries of a community drawn and what barriers to participation exist? Who sets the rules?

In HCI, the usage of the term often draws from participatory design and, as such, has to do with how end-users are involved in design processes (Vines et al., 2013) and scholars warn against falling into the trap of assuming it is an unqualified good (McCarthy and Wright, 2015). In the context of development projects, it has even been suggested that commitment to participation has gone so far beyond question and criticism that it constitutes a tyranny (Cooke and Kothari, 2001). In this chapter, though, rather than thinking about how communities are involved in shaping the design of exchange systems, the focus is on how and why community members do (or do not) take part in exchange activities once a system is in place. Attracting and fostering *participation* is an obvious concern for any socio-technical system designed to facilitate peer-to-peer activities—and so should be the closely related question of *inclusion*. Inclusion invites us to attend to factors that make it easy for some and difficult for others to take part.

Prior research has often addressed issues of trust, motivation, and critical mass to make sense of why some systems succeed in gaining traction while others struggle to foster activity over time (see Sidebox 6.1). While these are all fundamental to the dynamics of participation, we also need to account for more uncomfortable aspects of negotiating participation, such as discrimination and structural barriers that block some from reaping the benefits of participation. Moreover, alongside unwanted exclusion, peer-to-peer exchange has the tendency to include undesired inclusion. For example, when it comes to network hospitality, household members sometimes get drawn into hosting activities against their preferences (as discussed in the previous chapter), and stories of neighbors being impacted by the flow of Airbnb guests in their building abound (e.g., Gurran et al., 2020).

This chapter considers how participation is negotiated in the context of peer-to-peer exchange, drawing examples from network hospitality as well as local exchange arrangements for goods and services. The chapter is organized around three empirical examples: First, I address exclusion in the context of Airbnb, focusing in particular on how choices that lead to discriminatory outcomes can stem from homophily, the tendency of humans to seek the company of others who are similar to them.[7] Second, I discuss barriers to participation with an example of local peer-to-peer exchange where participants struggled to get involved due to being short on time and finding it hard to make room for sufficient relationship building.[8] Third, returning to the domain of network hospitality, I take on the question of unwanted inclusion and the implications others' exchange activities may have on individuals who have not chosen to be involved.[9]

### Sidebox 6.1: What does it take to participate?

When communities or companies are looking to set up an arrangement for peer-to-peer exchange, they must reckon with the question of how and why might people decide to get involved: What is in it for them? How will they hear about the system? What makes them curious enough to give it a try? And what does the system need to be like to appear trustworthy and credible enough to warrant any attention? Even the best online tools and assurance structures are meaningless if there is no one interested in using them.

---

[7] This section draws on research previously published in Ikkala and Lampinen (2014, 2015) and Lampinen and Cheshire (2016).

[8] This section draws on research previously published in Lampinen et al. (2015).

[9] This section draws on research previously published in Ikkala and Lampinen (2014, 2015), Lampinen (2014, 2016) and Lampinen and Cheshire (2016).

**Attracting and sustaining participation.** Setting up a peer-to-peer exchange system is, in part, a matter of attracting a critical mass (Markus, 1987) to "get the engine started": there needs to be many enough involved so that participants can match up with one another for meaningful exchanges. Rather than being solely a matter of numbers, however, the pool of participants needs to be diverse enough (Lampinen and Brown, 2017): An online marketplace where there are only people looking to buy and no sellers is an obvious no-go, so too a network hospitality platform full of guests but with no one to host them. Researchers have also considered paths of participation, aiming to better understand how participation can change over time and how, for instance, someone might go from lurking to active involvement in peer production (Balestra et al., 2016, 2017). These questions are crucial to all social computing technologies that rely on participants' activities and contributions to be meaningful. From attracting newcomers and retaining experienced members, to nurturing and encouraging different kinds of contributions, incentivizing participation is a long-standing challenge for Human–Computer Interaction (for a few examples, see, e.g., Antin, 2009; Harper et al., 2007; Kraut and Resnick, 2012; Ling et al., 2005; Preece and Shneiderman, 2009).

**Motivation.** Researchers have often approached participation with the lens of motivation (Lepper and Greene, 2015; Osterloh and Frey, 2000): *Extrinsic motivations* are those that can be satisfied through indirect compensation, such as money (Osterloh and Frey, 2000). *Intrinsic motivations* are a more direct form of compensation to meet one's immediate satisfaction or needs. They include a sense of achievement, completing tasks for their own sake, or for commitments associated with one's identity (Lepper and Greene, 2015). Motivations may be mixed both in that different participants are driven by different things and in that each participant may have various reasons for participation. As Bellotti et al. (Bellotti et al., 2015) put it, there is a muddle of motivations when it comes to peer-to-peer exchange. And while the initial spark to participate may be the possibility to make or save money—worthy goals in and of themselves—these do not preclude the possibility of more diverse motivations coming into play over time. For example, we ran into examples of this in a study on cooperatives (Lampinen et al., 2018): Interviewees explained how they had chosen to establish a cooperative as that was the cheapest and safest organizational structure available for them. In some cases, despite this purely pragmatic starting point, over time, those involved had grown to value the steer that cooperative principles gave to their activities.

**Trust**. Trust is often brought up as a crucial requirement for participation (Lauterbach et al., 2009; Rosen et al., 2011; Tan, 2010). The levels of risk and uncertainty, and with them the amount of interpersonal trust that is needed (or likely to come about) differ greatly. After all, interpersonal trust can only exist in the presence of risk and uncertainty (Cheshire, 2011; Cook et al., 2009). Here, it helps to differentiate between *perceived* and *actual risk*: simply "trusting someone" first does not make reality so. For example, while an individual may not perceive the potential risks and uncertainties in a personal relationship, those risks exist regardless of how much faith the person has that they will "be fine." Commitments can and do form because of the implicit or explicit acknowledgement of a desire to have a formalized relationship in a sea of other opportunities. If there were no risks (losing one's spouse) or uncertainties (whether the spouse's feelings could change over time) then there would be no need for commitments and promises in the first place. What is more, social research on trust-building processes demonstrates that trust typically develops in a gradual way as individuals take small risks with one another, and slowly increase the amount of risk over time (Cook et al., 2005). While people may cooperate with one another based merely on the expectation that the exchange partner will reciprocate and fulfill agreed-upon obligations, they develop trust only over time when cooperation is achieved, after they have experienced the person following through on promises and obligations. This means that trust is more likely to develop when it comes to repeated exchange with the same partner rather than one-off encounters.

## 6.1    WHO GETS LEFT OUT? HOMOPHILY AND DISCRIMINATORY OUTCOMES

Peer-to-peer exchange involves both in-person encounters and resources that people care about. As such, it is often relevant *who* one's exchange partner is. The more exchanges are framed around notions of community, sociability, or even friendship, the more those involved feel entitled to select with whom they engage. This is not very surprising—few would argue against the right to choose one's friends. However, peer-to-peer exchange is not always all that sociable. On the contrary, it can be quite transactional. This is where concerns around exclusion become visible: hotels are not free to discriminate in choosing their customers, so shouldn't the same apply to those who offer hospitality via platforms like Airbnb? On a continuum from intimate to impersonal, where does network hospitality land and what implications does (or should) that have for participation?

This section considers *homophily* and *discriminatory outcomes* in the context of network hospitality. Homophily—literally "the love of sameness"—is a sociological term that is relevant for considering the implications individuals' choices may have when it comes to participation and inclusion. Homophily refers to the tendency of individuals to associate and bond with similar others: birds of a feather flock together. The phenomenon is broadly known at least since the term was coined in the 1950s. It is somewhat ironic, though, that this tendency should come up in the context of network hospitality where meeting people with different cultural backgrounds is supposedly a central reason for participation. While hosts may be looking to experience a certain "strangeness," they often favor those who are in some way similar to them when they decide who to engage with (Molz, 2014). As such, the social encounters that network hospitality fosters may not be as inclusive and boundary-spanning as we might expect.

People's choices over who they wish to engage with may seem harmless in the first place, especially if we consider network hospitality more in terms of an interpersonal practice of hospitality than as a straightforward form of economic activity. However, the difference between innocuous personal preferences and harmful exclusion may be subtler than we would like to think. In the course of our research (Ikkala and Lampinen, 2015; Lampinen and Cheshire, 2016), hosts commonly highlighted tactics for attracting "like-minded" guests: Many of those we talked with both in Finland and in the U.S. reported that receiving many inquiries from potential guests gave them the opportunity to choose guests from a pool of candidates. Our participants' evaluations of potential guests were based on the guests' profiles, the reviews they had received from prior exchanges, and the communication that took place prior to accepting the accommodation request. They felt that viewing a guest's profile gave them insight into what kind of person the guest would be, and as Tomi explained, this allowed them to be intentional in choosing who to host: "*The fact that you can choose who comes there is nice. I just pretty much use my intuition in choosing the guests and try to choose guests who seem nice, you know, so that I might even spend some time with them if I feel like it.*" For their part, guests can, of course, make similar evaluations regarding potential hosts as they look for a place to stay. Some participants, such as Sophia, acknowledged this possibility and described how they had included a lot of information about themselves and their interests in their profiles in order to attract guests with whom they shared interests: "*I try to give a good picture of who I am in the profile because then the guest who is interested in staying at my place will likely be a kind of person whom I am interested in hosting. For example, I state here that I am not into drinking or smoking and that I really like to talk to people. And mostly the guests who end up at my place are quite similar to me.*"

The hosts we talked with appreciated being in control. For example, 22-year-old Kaisa, who sublet her room via Airbnb a few times a month—in addition to welcoming Couchsurfers every now and then—was eager to socialize with her guests. She wanted to do it in accordance with her own preferences, though, that is, only when she felt like it and only with guests who she found interesting. Efforts to attract certain types of guests and deter others were reflected in pricing tactics, too: As mentioned in Chapter 5, instead of always trying to find the optimal "market price," participants explained how they factored in social considerations, such as the type of guests they wished to host. Pricing became another means to assert control over hosting situations. Noteworthy here is that our research documents a period when the InstantBook feature that allows guests to book Airbnb stays without needing to get their request manually approved by the host was not yet available or much less common than it is at the time of this writing. Since our interviews, this feature has become much more prominent on the Airbnb platform (distancing it further from Couchsurfing) and it has been framed as one push on the part of Airbnb to deter discrimination.[10] Importantly, InstantBook streamlines the booking process, aligning Airbnb more closely with what one would expect at a hotel than when looking for an opportunity to couchsurf. This can take away from opportunities (or the need) to establish interpersonal trust. Moreover, while hosts may be less selective in who to host (trusting the platform to do sufficient vetting for them), this may be in part because the sociable aspects of network hospitality are becoming rarer.

In both Finland and the U.S., hosts reported making efforts to increase the likelihood of an enjoyable encounter by deliberately selecting guests they expected to be easy to host. And who did they think would fit that bill? Often, the preference was for individuals who resembled the host in some respect. Having common ground with guests was seen to improve the odds of interesting interactions, such as in 31-year-old Sami's comment about educational attainment and the lines of work guests were engaged in: "*For the most part, our guests have been highly educated and they are in interesting jobs. They are the kind of people with whom it is easy for us to find some common ground, and, therefore, the conversations have often been very interesting.*" Of course, this is not always the case: Some hosts are fairly indifferent to who their guests are. Others have been documented to purposefully break the pattern of like-mindedness in an effort to keep things interesting: these experienced couchsurfers "engineer randomness" and embrace encounters that they expect to be more boundary spanning and even awkward (Bialski, 2012a; Molz, 2014). The tendency to look for and choose guests who are similar to the host or who share the host's interests is understandable when we focus on the interpersonal aspects of network hospitality. After all, already the classic sociologist Simmel (1903/1950) saw similarity and equal social standing of the interacting parties as a central condition for sociable interaction. Yet, this tendency to homophily is also at the root of discriminatory outcomes in network hospitality.

More drastically, some participants openly described refusing potential guests because they were members of particular racial, ethnic, or age groups. Gender came up, too, especially in some female hosts' hesitations to host men who were travelling alone. A few stated that they did not wish to host people from specific countries. For instance, Sophia explained that, because of previous bad experiences of subletting, she chose not to host people from India or "*black people.*" She went on to explain that she knew that this kind of selectivity is "*not a good thing*" but that she knowingly did it anyway, on account of her prior negative experiences. Similarly, a number of the hosts we talked with in Finland stated that they were "*maybe a bit more selective*" when it came to accepting Russian

---

[10]  https://www.marketplace.org/2016/09/08/airbnb-thinks-increased-instant-bookings-will-curb-discrimination/ (read on June 4, 2021)

guests. As one might expect in an interview setting, like Ida in the following excerpt, many went on to express awareness that this kind of discriminatory behavior is problematic, explaining how they tried to avoid practicing it: "*Well, if I think about who we have declined most, they're probably Russian people. We've hosted Russian guests, but still I notice that I think twice before I accept. It's a big and diverse country, and I know I shouldn't think this way, but still...*" While individual hosts may apply group-based heuristics in an effort to achieve enjoyable encounters, learn from past experiences, or to manage risks, when taken together, such considerations can produce discriminatory outcomes. No harm intended does not necessarily equal no harm done.

Mounting research highlights the prevalence of discrimination in online marketplaces: As one example, Edelman and Luca (2014) identified racial bases of discrimination among Airbnb users in the U.S. In their experimental study, they found that non-black hosts were able to charge 12% more than black hosts for comparable accommodations, controlling for all other information available on the Airbnb listings. When people are at a freedom to choose who they exchange with, and when they are provided with "digital trust infrastructure" (Sundararajan, 2016), such as profiles with photos and reviews left by prior exchange partners, to guide those decisions, the resulting choices can reveal ugly social dynamics. As Lingel (2020) has pointed out, mechanisms that are intended for fostering trust can end up enabling racism and discrimination.

Network hospitality may work well for many people most of the time, but when considering the implications of these and other exchange arrangements, we need to consider those who have a disproportionately hard time participating or are outright excluded from participation due to their race, age, gender, or other characteristics. How do these systems affect them? How might they be redesigned so as to promote anti-discriminatory outcomes? In a book on how the internet and new digital technologies—in particular smartphones and social media—shape what it is like to come of age in poor, minority, inner city communities, Lane (2018) draws attention to the fact that much of the research on context collapse and boundary regulation has focused on the kinds of risks commonly faced by middle-class and racially privileged youth, like embarrassment, while for less privileged youth, the concerns revolve around safety, violence, and adverse encounters with law enforcement. Similarly, when it comes to network hospitality, early academic accounts have largely overlooked particularly troubling experiences, even though the emergence of alternative systems like Innclusive and Fairbnb, along with the experiences shared via hashtags like #airbnbwhileblack, make it very obvious that the most visible systems are not working out equally well for everyone.

## 6.2 MOTIVATION ALONE IS NOT ENOUGH

Even when no one is actively—or mindlessly—excluding potential participants, there may be barriers to participation that keep people out despite their interest in peer-to-peer exchange and the benefits participation could bring. When you hear the word *scarcity*, you probably think of money, but it is not the only resource that may be necessary for participation. This section considers how scarcity of time or other resources can constrain opportunities to get involved in peer-to-peer exchange. It tells the story of a single parents' community in the U.S. that was trying to set up their own instance of the peer-to-peer exchange system Kassi. Next to outlining how individuals' motivation is not always enough to enable their participation, I will also reflect on how exchange arrangements might be best set up so as to facilitate successful matches between exchange partners. Having a need for the resources that an exchange arrangement could deliver and being motivated to reap the benefits of participation is not always enough for bringing about the desired outcomes.

## 6.2.1   SCARCITY TRAP

Even when participation does not necessitate direct financial investment, other requirements may inhibit the adoption of a peer-to-peer exchange system. When it came to the single parents' community we studied in the U.S., such requirements included the initial social commitment and time investment to build trusted relationships and embrace a new online system (Lampinen et al., 2015). In this case, pressures related to the specific local context (e.g., single parenthood) impeded opportunities to engage in peer-to-peer exchange, even when members of the network viewed the social and material benefits of participation as desirable or even necessary. The risks and uncertainties in this community were evident: the single parents were most interested in exchanges that directly involved their own children, such as carpools, childcare, and playdates. This brings up an irony that is central to peer-to-peer exchange in local settings: When the stakes are low (e.g., second-hand goods like children's clothing), participation may not feel worth the effort required to handle the logistics. When stakes are high, participation may feel too risky (e.g., in-person encounters like child care) unless those involved have a pre-existing trust relationship—and the construction of trust relationships takes time and energy, as they are typically built from lower-stake exchanges and repeated interactions over time.

Network members wanted to reduce risk and uncertainty through direct, face-to-face interpersonal interaction before engaging in technology-mediated exchanges. Since they preferred to rely on face-to-face interactions and social activities as vetting mechanisms for who they felt comfortable with and who they deemed trustworthy, they found that it was exceedingly difficult to gradually build social ties and foster interpersonal trust in the midst of their demanding daily lives. It would have taken time together to build up trusting relationships, but making time for anything beyond the daily necessities was a challenge for many of the participants. Yet, such strong ties were deemed necessary preconditions for the higher-risk exchanges that the network members were interested in. While the desire for face-to-face interaction as a prerequisite for online interaction may not be typical of most exchange arrangements, establishing some level of interpersonal trust is relevant for all local peer-to-peer exchange communities. When we contrast this case with our earlier work on local online exchange in our student community in Finland (Lampinen et al., 2013;

Suhonen et al., 2010), it is clear that the benefits and risks related to participation may be weighed very differently across diverse social contexts.

Managing multiple responsibilities and struggling with time management were common challenges among interviewees. Many faced financial challenges, too. The high cost of child care and the need to work long hours in order to earn enough was sometimes an overwhelming combination. These factors meant that community members struggled to make the most of scarce resources also when it came to accessing support from the network. This echoes Mullainathan and Shafir's (2013) definition of the scarcity trap where one ends up having even less than one could have, due to always being one step behind and juggling to get by—both of which contribute to one's scarcity. Members of the network struggled to get involved in peer-to-peer exchange due to being short on time and finding it hard to make room for sufficient relationship building. For example, not having child care available made it hard to join social events with other community members that, over time, could have allowed for collaborative child care arrangements. In other words, the single parents in this community were short on the same resources that they would have liked to access through the network. This made it difficult for them to get more actively involved and partake in the benefits that a supportive peer community could have offered.

## 6.2.2    MATCHING ISSUES

While individuals' circumstances are central to their participation, ultimately peer-to-peer exchange arrangements flourish or fail on the level of the community: an individual may be as motivated and capable of contributing as imaginable and, yet, if there aren't sufficiently many other people interested, that alone does little to make an exchange community work. Exchange arrangements can work only if they succeed in attracting sufficient participation. However, numbers alone are not enough: the participant pool also needs to be one where meaningful matches can come about (Lampinen and Brown, 2017). If everyone is offering the same thing and looking for the same thing, it may be impossible even for a large group of people to barter successfully. Rather, then, we need to consider who can collaborate with whom meaningfully.

Matching like with like can be problematic from an inclusion point of view, but when activities are shaped around the notion of peer support—as was the case in the single parents' community—some level of common ground is crucial. Needless to say, this need not require demographic similarity in terms of race, gender, or age. The members of the network we collaborated with were all single parents. The shared experience of being a single parent was intended to be the glue that would turn the network into an ongoing, supportive community. The founder of the network, a single mother with two young sons, envisioned the network as an opportunity to facilitate the everyday lives of single parents in her local area. In her conception, the network was meant to help meet several goals, including discussing emotions and thoughts with peers, gaining knowledge regarding parenting, sharing material resources, and simply fighting the isolation associated with single parenting.

Next to a shared status as single parents, interviewees shared a desire for peer support. Beneath the veneer of shared experience, however, we discovered an astonishing diversity regarding the community members' demographics, life situations, and histories of becoming a single parent. While all network members we talked with had a desire for peer support as a single parent, their lived experiences were not always similar enough to enable them to be peers to the degree that they would have hoped. When it came to arranging peer-to-peer exchange of goods and services, however, another issue emerged: the participants were not well positioned to help each other since they were all struggling with a scarcity of time. Here, matching participants with one another for meaningful exchange arrangements was difficult. It might have been necessary to reconsider the pool of participants to overcome the issue. As a hypothetical example, perhaps there would have been elderly people residing in the vicinity who would have had ample time to spare and for whom interactions with local children would have been more than welcome.

## 6.3    UNWANTED INCLUSION OF RELUCTANT PERIPHERAL PARTICIPANTS

In addition to those actively—and voluntarily—involved, peer-to-peer exchange activities often end up drawing in or impacting a number of others, including household members, neighbors, and more broadly residents in neighborhoods where such activities are frequent. Considering reluctant peripheral participants and other indirect stakeholders impacted by peer-to-peer exchange illustrates another wrinkle in straightforward stories of participation (which have been challenged also in prior HCI, for instance, by distinguishing between witting and unwitting participation (Vines et al., 2013)). It also brings up further concerns regarding fair outcomes, as peripheral participants are less likely to reap the benefits of participation that those actively involved in peer-to-peer exchange seek. To illustrate these issues, we return to the example of network hospitality: both Airbnb and Couchsurfing involve a rich set of actors beyond the host and the guest.

Let's start considering peripheral participation by returning to the case of individuals getting pulled into hosting activities by their more enthusiastic household members (see Chapter 5). Most research on network hospitality has focused on the dynamics of host–guest relationships, with the occasional remark that encounters do not necessarily take place between one host and one guest (Bialski, 2012b; Buchberger, 2012): people often share their homes with others who may get involved in hosting more or less voluntarily. Bialski (2012a) has noted how introducing guests to domestic spaces *"can cause unease to those who normally have a lot of control over that space,"* such as household members who have not been alerted to a guest's arrival or who are unaware of the context or conditions of a visit. Hosts do not always keep those they live with up-to-date on their plans around network hospitality. This can cause conflicts within the household. Bialski (2012b) shares an example of a Canadian couchsurfer named Oliver whose introduction to his host's home caused unease to another household member: "*It was [Maricka's] first time hosting anyone. So, she met me at the train station at 7am which was really nice. And then she dropped me off at her house and she gave me a little bed. And what she didn't tell me is that she hadn't explained to her grandmother, who was living there, that I was going to come. And her grandmother couldn't speak any English or French. And so [my host] left to go to work, and her grand-mother woke up an hour later and she saw me, and she started having like this heaving fit. Like this [demonstrates] and apparently she has this breathing disorder. But I thought that she was going to take the big one right there from me not being able to explain who I am and I'm just this strange person in her house. And so I tried to explain through hand signals which just didn't work. And then I was just like, time to leave, I'll just come back later. So, I went to lock the door behind me because [Maricka] had given me a key. And the grandmother saw me and came up behind me heaving and grabbed the key and went back into her room ... And later on when Maricka explained who I was the grand-mother was very happy to see me. Patting me on the head.*"

Considering unwanted inclusion also opens up the question of who benefits from participation. From the examples covered in this book, it seems that the immediate benefits—be it in the form of enjoyable social encounters, "reputational capital," or making money—largely fall on those directly involved. Out of all different types of peripheral participants, household members are the ones most likely to share both the upsides and downsides of participation: while they may not have sought to become hosts, they might well find the resulting social interactions fun or interesting, and when it comes to Airbnb where hosting results in additional income, there is a chance that they will benefit from it in some way, too. Where the household members in our studies did host together, however, it remained an open question whether and how everyone would get to benefit from the online reputation that was gained by hosting (Lampinen, 2014).

Second, let us turn to actors outside the participating household(s). Molz' (2014) suggestion to consider encounters between hosts and guests as *co-production* helpfully highlights how the roles of guest and host get blurred into a collaborative activity where everyone makes hospitable gestures. Importantly for the discussion here, it makes room for accounting for the broader network of actors, ranging from family members and housemates to travel partners, neighbors, and beyond, who are impacted by home-stays and who may play a role in enabling or inhibiting them. As one example, Buchberger's (2012) research depicts how receiving foreign members of the Couchsurfing community is possible only against great odds in Morocco: It involves various risks, including potential for trouble with the police. In this context, the practice of hospitality exchange is subversive. Inviting foreign tourists to one's home or simply walking in the street in the company of a foreign-looking person can attract surveillance, lead to being stopped by "tourist police" officers, and even result in being imprisoned for two nights. Yet, despite these disconcerting possibilities, most Moroccan CouchSurfers in Buchberger's study were more concerned about a different difficulty and obstacle for hosting: the fear of gossip among neighbors and the conflicts with their family and landlords that their activities might cause.

When it comes to Airbnb, one need not look far to find accounts of landlords and neighbors taking issue with frequent hosting activities (e.g., Gurran et al., 2020; Gurran and Phibbs, 2017). Neighbors and more broadly people in the neighborhood are also less likely to benefit from others' peer-to-peer exchange activities. To the degree that neighbors are aware and involved, it most often falls upon them to tolerate the guests in their building, without getting social or economic benefits in return. Similarly, when tenants wanted to host, they made efforts to keep the landlord out of the picture. These latter groups are less participants to the peer-to-peer exchange and more stakeholders who are impacted by others' activities: the feel of a residential building changes if one or more of the units is used more as a hotel than as a home. More broadly, when professionalized, network hospitality can impact entire neighborhoods by bringing in flows of tourism that traditionally have not been part of their everyday. As Nieuwland and van Melik (2020) point out, neighborhoods can profit from increased attention and income, but more commonly network hospitality is disruptive to the traditional lodging industry and it can trigger gentrification processes where housing affordability and availability are jeopardized when housing units are turned into vacation rentals.

## 6.4    CONCLUSION

So how might we better address issues of participation and inclusion when designing for peer-to-peer exchange? Peer-to-peer exchange systems are also faced with the fact that different people are looking to get different things out of a particular exchange or their overall participation. Accommodating this can be a challenge, especially when an exchange arrangement has been set up with a clear ideological drive, such as promoting environmental sustainability, or when it is driven by a particular vision of communal interaction that builds up relational assets. Yet, as the founder of a tool bank in Edinburgh put it in introducing their activities,[11] it may be best to not worry about *why* people are joining, as long as they are participating in an appropriate way.

When thinking about participation, an important starting point is to recognize the central requirements in different types of exchange. To encourage participation—and support negotiations over its conditions—we need to reflect on participation both on the level of individuals and communities and to attend to the different types of exchange at play. When it comes to thinking about participation in peer-to-peer exchange, it is integral to keep in mind that 'sharing' in this domain is diverse and one size certainly does not fit all. The requirements for participation are different in different types of exchange: Quite obviously, what is being exchanged matters: Are the participants dealing with physical goods and if so, how do they handle the logistics? If the goods exchanged are low value, participants may ask themselves whether the exchange is worth the effort it takes. Or

---

[11]    http://sharingandcaring.eu/news/visit-edinburgh-tools-library (read on June 4, 2021)

is the exchange rather about a service, such as some window cleaning offered via a time bank, and if so, what might participants need to avoid feelings of indebtedness or being taken advantage of? In some cases, exchanges might be best understood as co-productions (Carroll, 2013; Molz, 2014) and that, too, places some requirements on what appropriate participation looks like. On a related note, the stakes for participants may range from low to very high. Just think of the contrast between gifting away a piece of furniture you no longer need and trusting someone to look after your child or pet for a few hours. An irony of peer-to-peer exchange is that when the stakes are low, participation may not feel worthwhile, but when the stakes are high enough to motivate participation, it can feel too risky to get involved.

Exchanges may also be either one-off or repeated. This has repercussions for what is necessary in terms of trust and what is to be expected in terms of sociability. In repeated exchange, role reversal may take place over time, such as when a couchsurfer ends up offering hospitality to a person who has hosted them previously. Moreover, while it sometimes does not matter much what one's exchange partner is like—beyond a bare minimum of getting the exchange completed without getting hurt or scammed—in other cases, such as when sharing a home temporarily, people care deeply about who they will stumble upon in the morning as they are looking for the day's first cup of coffee. In these types of cases people often look for "like-minded" exchange partners and the expectation of seeing eye to eye with someone serves as a basis of trusting the exchange partner (Molz, 2014; Ikkala and Lampinen, 2015). In cases like this, where there is an emphasis on sociability and interpersonal trust, we should watch out for how homophily—the tendency of people to prefer engaging with others who are similar to them—can lead to discriminatory outcomes.

While individuals need to be motivated to participate in peer-to-peer exchange, that alone does not guarantee that an exchange arrangement will succeed in sustaining activity or ensuring equitable opportunities for participation. Individuals' motivation is of little help if there are structural barriers blocking their participation, such as scarcity traps or community-level dynamics that make it unlikely for participants to find others well matched to exchange with them. First, for high-stakes exchanges, interpersonal trust is needed—and establishing trust relationships takes time and effort. Second, next to how limited economic means can quite obviously prohibit participation—you can't book an Airbnb rental without a credit card—scarcity in terms of time and energy can lead to exclusion from participation. Third, on the community level, the right mix of participants needs to be in place to make things work. Matching like with like can be socially tempting, but it may introduce problems in terms of what each participant can bring into the exchange and how likely the participants are well positioned to cooperate with one another.

Finally, we must consider unwanted inclusion and the implications that exchange activities have on indirect stakeholders. When analyzing and designing exchange platforms, we need to look beyond the single individual as the user (or focusing narrowly on the host–guest dyad) and reckon with the social and economic implications of social computing technologies. Baumber et al. (2019)

have proposed thinking about community acceptance in terms of "a social license" to operate, referring to a way of both conceptualizing and strategically building approval for emerging sharing activities that goes beyond the requirements of a formal regulatory process. This is one promising approach for considering appropriate policy and community responses to peer-to-peer exchange and its implications on various indirect stakeholders.

# CHAPTER 7

# Future Directions

*"As we start to understand better how markets and marketplaces work,
we realize that we can intervene in them, redesign them, fix them when they're broken,
and start new ones where they will be useful."*

— Alvin E. Roth in *Who Gets What—and Why*

This book has outlined and explored interpersonal challenges that hinder peer-to-peer exchange. I have noted continuously how these challenges are not easily solvable and how there certainly is no simple technological fix for them. This requires us to ask what we can hope to accomplish with the help of further research and design in this domain. There are several future directions to choose from: First, we might think of ways to redesign existing digital *platforms* or come up with altogether new platforms. Second, we could take a service design perspective, reshaping the whole *experience* of taking part in platform-mediated peer-to-peer exchange. Third, though closely related to the first two, we might think of ways to redesign the *markets* that platforms support, perhaps with the help of lessons learned from economics. While all of these are relevant, what I will focus on in the final pages of this book are the fundamental interpersonal tensions that limit the uptake of exchange platforms and stall the flourishing of peer-to-peer exchange. Summing up lessons learned from a decade of research on peer-to-peer exchange, this chapter focuses on what we need to keep in mind when we work to support negotiations regarding reciprocity, closeness, and participation.

Given the challenges that have been brought up in this book, we must also ask whether the sharing economy has been a failure: Is the story of peer-to-peer oriented exchange arrangements a narrative of misplaced hope and failed efforts? If so, why bother investing our energies into studying the domain and designing for it? Echoing María Puig de la Bellacasa's (2017) writing, I suggest that we need to acknowledge the poisons in our grounds and keep going: It would be naïve and harmful to pretend that everything is going as well as initially hoped for and promised. At the same time, peer-to-peer exchange still holds potential as a path to envisioning systemic responses to systemic crises—social, economic, and environmental. Rather than abandoning efforts at studying and designing for peer-to-peer exchange, I join Juliet Schor's (2020) call for reclaiming the sharing economy: There is much that is problematic in how the phenomenon has unfolded. With full acknowledgment of its problems and challenges, I argue that flourishing peer-to-peer exchange is *possible* and that it can be *worthwhile*. To reorient our thinking in this way, I propose, first, considering failures as worthy objects of study in and of themselves and, second, revisiting our criteria of success.

Finally, the future directions I propose require us to bring into dialogue strands of thinking that seem, at first, unlikely bedfellows. First, research in economics, and in particular market design (Roth, 2008, 2015), can serve our efforts to study existing markets, design new exchange arrangements, and evaluate design choices. Second, in exploring the sharing economy critically and seeking to create hopeful alternatives to the status quo, we can turn to approaches, such as Design Justice (Costanza-Chock, 2020), that aim explicitly to challenge, rather than reproduce, structural inequalities.

## 7.1    LESSONS LEARNED REGARDING RECIPROCITY AND INDEBTEDNESS

For a peer-to-peer exchange arrangement to flourish, it has to be organized so that those participating get something of value out of their involvement. Be it a system like Airbnb that is built around transactions or an arrangement that relies on generalized reciprocity in the spirit of Couchsurfing, exchange always involves some type of reciprocation. Monetary transactions can go a long way in giving exchange partners the means to even things out. For most people, they are the most familiar framework for exchange. Yet, as illustrated in Chapter 4, the value that is being exchanged may be much more nuanced than just money in exchange for goods or services. What an exchange partner gets out of participation can range from reputational benefits to meaningful interpersonal interaction or—as is the case when it comes to giving away items via systems like Freecycle—the convenience of getting rid of unwanted possessions that clutter the house. Where monetary transacting is explicitly banned or otherwise deemed inappropriate—such as in Couchsurfing or a timebank—participants need other means for reciprocation and for alleviating feelings of indebtedness. Without appropriate reciprocation, exchanges risk being experienced as unfair and relationships may erode quickly (Emerson, 1972a, 1972b). In order to design exchange arrangements in ways that are mindful of the challenges of reciprocity, we need to understand the situationally varying social norms that guide exchange processes as well as participants' expectations regarding rules of engagement in exchange processes.

**Exchange experiences are always shaped by how reciprocation is handled.** Emphasizing direct, negotiated transactions can make exchange processes straightforward but distant. This is the most familiar model of balancing things out so as to accomplish an exchange that is experienced as fair and orderly. When the aim is to forego (or discourage) the use of money, direct reciprocity may be hard to organize—matching people for direct barter is difficult, especially in small networks. Simultaneously, indirect, generalized reciprocity can feel awkward for those not accustomed to it. This means that any system that hopes to promote indirect forms of reciprocity should make special efforts to facilitate new participants' paths to engagement.

**Participants may need help in learning new modes of reciprocation.** One should not assume that participants are familiar with something like the logic of generalized exchange or that they have sufficient experience of these types of exchanges to feel at ease with them. If people are used to being treated as *customers*, there is no reason to assume they know how to (or are willing to make the effort to) change roles and act as *community members*, instead. Even when potential participants believe in the value of community, they may need guidance with how to foster one.

**Freeriding is a problem to watch out for, but so is stagnation due to fears of indebtedness (or of being perceived as a greedy or less than charitable person).** Fear of indebtedness can make any exchange situation fraught. This is the necessary flipside of the norm of reciprocity: it does not feel good to feel indebted to another person. Moreover, anything that can be interpreted as *helping* can introduce a power dynamic that may be uncomfortable or outright problematic. In this vein, distinct participation roles can become troublesome, especially if they are framed around giving and receiving or helping and receiving help. Co-production (Carroll, 2013; Molz, 2014) can be a more helpful framing.

**Communicating and managing expectations is key for navigating reciprocity.** Given the double fears of indebtedness and freeloading, online exchange systems should, first, communicate clearly what kinds of behavior is expected and, second, encourage participants to align their expectations with their exchange partners as clearly and early as possible. Given how familiar the role of a customer now is to most people, expanding potential users' horizons to other modes of exchange and engagement might necessitate a nudge. Should participants expect to receive comparable benefits for their contributions? Or are they expected to act out of a general concern for their community members, benefiting those in need when in a position to do so? To avoid confusion, expectations regarding exchange should be clarified beyond the vague idea of *sharing* with a community. This can help participants avoid mismatched expectations and the troubles they may introduce.

**Modes of exchange blend into one another.** Even when there is an understanding for a direct, negotiated exchange, and when the agreed-upon payment has been taken care of via an exchange platform, there are still acts of reciprocation that are needed to manage the exchange encounter interactionally. For instance, when it comes to Airbnb, this may involve performing the roles of a good host and a good guest. Similarly, when no direct payment is expected and reciprocity is to work out over time on the level of the community, like in Couchsurfing, this does not mean that the exchange partners would not also acknowledge and manage debts of gratitude directly between themselves.

**It is possible to design purposefully with different modes of exchange to foster desired social qualities.** A crucial challenge for design is to find ways to alleviate the discomfort of indebtedness without doing away with the norm of reciprocity. In striving to encourage activity by making participation more convenient, we need to be attentive to what social qualities may get removed in the process. Having to make an effort can constitute a barrier to activity, but it is integral to fostering particular social and relational outcomes (Light and Miskelly, 2019). Convenience alone is not an appropriate goal when the broader vision of an exchange arrangement exceeds consumption—one cannot buy community.

## 7.2   LESSONS LEARNED REGARDING CLOSENESS AND INTIMACY

Interpersonal encounters are necessarily vulnerable and effortful. As trust scholars argue, interpersonal trust can only exist in the presence of risk and uncertainty (Cheshire, 2011; Cook et al., 2009). The presence of risk and uncertainty is integral to experiences of vulnerability in peer-to-peer exchange—and peer-to-peer exchange has the capacity to foster meaningful closeness and a sense of community exactly because it requires participants to get involved without assurances of how the encounter will unfold. Inconvenient as it may be, it is impossible to do away with initial feelings of vulnerability and still achieve experiences of intimacy. When appropriate for the overall values of a system, designers can leverage financial exchange and reliable brokering systems to alleviate some of the uncertainty that participation involves. Finally, we should be mindful that exchange partners are not always looking for close, sociable interactions. Peer-to-peer exchange does not need to lead to closeness between the exchange partners.

**Exchanges differ drastically from one another.** As a starting point, we need to be attentive to the kind of exchange processes we are working with. The social dynamics involved can differ drastically: It is one thing for Couchsurfing hosts and guests to experience momentary closeness, knowing that after the encounter they do not need to see each other ever again unless they specifically choose to stay in touch. It is another thing entirely for neighbors to foster a sense of closeness, with the knowledge that if things were to sour, they would still be stuck with one another in their everyday setting. When we design for different types of peer-to-peer exchange, we need to find ways to be sensitive to the intentions and concerns that shape exchange encounters.

**Closeness in social encounters, including peer-to-peer exchange, requires effort.** Accomplishing closeness in a peer-to-peer encounter requires mutual effort from those involved. Even when exchange partners are open for social encounters, they may not want them enough to put in the effort that would be needed for accomplishing a sense of closeness. Participants' effort matters beyond its direct outcomes within a particular exchange: the necessity of making an effort is central for the creation of relational assets (Light and Miskelly, 2019)—the social benefits that emerge over time from local sharing initiatives and support solidarity, making further initiatives more likely to succeed. To foster desired social qualities, we may need to nudge those involved to do the work that their preferred outcomes require, regardless of whether the aim is to uphold a sense of distance characteristic of impersonal transacting or to foster a more intimate connection akin to an encounter with a friend.

**Exchange partners' desires for closeness do not always match.** Attempts at closeness may feel very awkward when encounters do not play out in line with what those involved expected from one another. In opening up for the possibility of interpersonal trust and social connection, exchange partners have to take some risk, even if the potential adverse outcome may not be more than slight embarrassment. When it comes to designing for peer-to-peer exchange, though, we must also reckon with the less common cases where things go seriously wrong. In such situations, the adverse outcomes of a peer-to-peer encounter can be much worse, including violations of physical and psychological safety. Following the design justice approach (Costanza-Chock, 2020), we might ask these three important questions: Who participated in the design process? Who benefited from the design? And who was harmed by the design?

**Money can facilitate participation and help us draw in cautious newcomers.** When introduced into peer-to-peer exchange, money does more than allow participants to even things out. It carries deep social meaning, and it can be put to serve social ends, such as selecting exchange partners and managing their expectations. In interpersonal terms, there need not to exist a contradiction between monetary and social motives for participation. When appropriate for the overall values of a system, designers can leverage financial exchange and reliable brokering systems to alleviate some of the uncertainty that participation involves. This can help attract and retain participants who are cautious about peer-to-peer exchange and therefore less likely to engage in interactions that they deem risky.

**Face-to-face interaction is not the only possible form of closeness.** The distinction between *online* and *offline* as separate spheres of life remains persistent in everyday discourse, often in a way that continues to position face-to-face encounters as the (implicit) gold standard for assessing social interaction and experiences of closeness. We should be mindful that while in-person encounters can be one of the main selling points of peer-to-peer exchange, the desired social qualities vary depending on the type of exchange and the people involved. In designing systems for peer-to-peer exchange, it is not wise to assume that the kind of closeness that can come about in face-to-face interaction should (or could) always characterize successful peer-to-peer exchange.

**Respecting desires to retain social distance can open up fruitful avenues for design.** When it comes to peer-to-peer exchange, sometimes people want to keep those around them— be it neighbors or more fleeting exchange partners like guests looking for a place to stay—at a comfortable distance, without seeming rude or uncongenial. While addressing the desire to retain social distance can seem misanthropic, it might prove fruitful to explore how we might design for social distance. Rather than evaluating all peer-to-peer technologies based on their ability to foster deep and long-lasting connections, we might aim at facilitating connections that involve low commitment and/or little effort. Prior work suggests that this could support meaningful and helpful exchanges, respond to desires to live in a community where there is a generalized sense of trust and friendliness, and help encourage and communicate such sentiments (Lampinen et al., 2017).

**Design choices impact on the social qualities that a system promotes.** While participants always need to play their part in making an exchange work, it is possible to design systems in ways that remove some of the effort involved in peer-to-peer exchange (as illustrated in the example of how arranging a stay works on Airbnb vs on Couchsurfing). Yet, beyond differing outcomes in terms of efficiency, such choices impact on the social qualities that a system promotes. The most effective solution may not be the one that best serves the values that we are seeking to support through design. We need to hold ourselves and platform companies accountable: in designing platforms and other exchange arrangements, we make value choices when shaping the interactional space available for those involved in peer-to-peer exchange.

## 7.3    LESSONS LEARNED REGARDING PARTICIPATION AND INCLUSION

Encouraging participation in peer-to-peer exchange—and supporting negotiations over its conditions—requires us to reflect on both the level of individuals and communities. First, trying to reduce participation into a question of motivation is insufficient. Motivation is obviously of importance: if potential participants are not interested and see no reason to get involved, there is little point in setting up an exchange arrangement for them. But even when participants would be motivated to participate, motivation alone may not be enough to ensure that they actually can and will get involved. Individuals' motivation is of little help if there are structural barriers blocking their participation, such as scarcity traps or community-level dynamics that make it unlikely for participants to find people well matched to exchange with them at the right time. Second, where there is an emphasis on sociability and interpersonal trust, participation may be hindered by discriminatory outcomes that are connected to homophily (tendency of people to prefer engaging with others who are similar to them). Third, beyond the issue of how to get people on board, we should also consider how to allow them to refrain from involvement. When it comes to the challenges with participation, unwanted inclusion and the implications exchange activities have on a range of indirect stakeholders are part of the issue.

**The type of exchange shapes the requirements that are central for participation.** The challenges involved in one-off exchanges with relatively low stakes, like buying or selling used goods, are very different from those in high-stakes, repeated exchanges that necessitate long-term relationships, such as joining forces with a neighbor to arrange childcare or carpooling. The levels of risk and the amount of interpersonal trust that is needed differ greatly between different types of exchange arrangements, too—one size does not fit all. This might be one explanation for why so many systems that have been set up for local online exchange have failed to gain traction: catering to all kinds of exchanges at once risks leading to a solution that does not work well for any particular type (perhaps with the notable exception of Craigslist which, of course, has challenges of its own

(Lingel, 2020)). Rather than aiming to support peer-to-peer exchange writ large, then, a narrower scope could be a more productive place to start.

While individual motivation matters, scarcity may prevent participation. Beyond the obvious constraints that limited economic means pose, scarcity of time and energy can make participation prohibitively difficult, even for participants who find the benefits of participation attractive and meaningful. How might design help participants avoid being blocked by a scarcity trap (Mullainathan and Shafir, 2013) where one ends up having even less than one could have, due to always being one step behind and juggling to get by—both of which contribute to one's scarcity?

**Rather than just a critical mass in terms of number of participants, peer-to-peer exchange necessitates the right mix of participants.** While matching like with like can be socially tempting, it may also be problematic in terms of what each participant can bring into the exchange. To make meaningful matches, there need to be participants who have complementary skills and needs. In market design terms, markets can suffer from an oversupply on one side (such as too many buyers in comparison to the number of sellers), or a lack of good enough matches to convince participants to stay in the marketplace (e.g., it is not enough for Airbnb guests that accommodation is on offer in their destination but some offers need to match their preferences). Where peer-to-peer exchange has the characteristic of being a two-sided market (such as featuring hosts and guests), encouraging participants to alternate between both roles increases the number of potential matches, without necessarily requiring a larger overall number of participants. Moreover, conveying signs of activity and evidence of emerging norms is important when the aim is to encourage participation and "get the engine started."

**The tendency to prefer interacting with those similar to oneself results in discriminatory outcomes in peer-to-peer exchange.** While people may consider themselves truly motivated to meet new people through participation in peer-to-peer exchange, they often prefer to engage with others who are similar to them in some, or many, ways. This may seem innocuous enough at a glance: Choosing to be with people with whom one has some common ground is not unreasonable, nor is wanting to choose with whom one shares intimacies. Yet, this tendency to homophily is also at the root of discriminatory outcomes in network hospitality and presumably peer-to-peer exchange more broadly. The situation can be made worse by *digital trust infrastructure* (Sundararajan, 2016), such as personal profiles and reviews from prior exchange partners. These features have been deemed central to the functioning of peer-to-peer systems but their implications are different for different people. When considering the implications of these and other features, we need to consider those who have a disproportionately hard time participating or are outright excluded from participation due to their race, age, gender, or other characteristics. How do different features affect their experience? And how might these features be redesigned so as to promote anti-discriminatory outcomes?

**Peer-to-peer exchange can feature unwanted inclusion.** It can have implications for a range of indirect stakeholders, including household members, neighbors, and residents of entire neighborhoods that are affected by emerging patterns of peer-to-peer activity. This is a domain where there is a clear need to go beyond the traditional design focus on "the user" and direct stakeholders. To reckon with the social and economic implications of peer-to-peer exchange arrangements, designers can turn to existing approaches, such as Value-Sensitive Design (Friedman and Hendry, 2019) and Design Justice (Costanza-Chock, 2020), that center values in design and ask challenging questions about who is benefiting and who is being harmed.

## 7.4   STUDYING FAILURE AND REVISITING CRITERIA FOR SUCCESS

While there has been much enthusiasm regarding neighborly sharing practices and the co-use of underutilized resources, these practices have not become the mainstream successes that the early hype anticipated them to become. Rather than lamenting this state of affairs or choosing to focus only on the few platforms that have become household names, we can consider failures as worthy objects of study and revisit our criteria of what constitutes success.

**Many sharing initiatives never really took off or were abandoned after a short existence. Yet, we should recognize and respect the small victories that many such failures involve.** People tried to make something happen for themselves, some exchanges got made, and even if a particular initiative did not last, the experiences, relationships, and ideas it brought about may still have shaped the future (even if only in small ways). Failures are worthy objects of study as they can teach us to do things differently the next time around: A good understanding of why things fell apart—or perhaps more fairly, why the outcome was different from what was expected—can be highly useful for future work.

**Over time, documenting what was tried—and what did not work out—in particular settings can reveal interpersonal and community level dynamics that repeat across contexts.** The issues around reciprocity we identified in the Finnish student community may look a little different for another type of exchange arrangement, but the fundamental questions come up over and over again. Similarly, scarcity as an obstacle to the involvement of highly motivated participants will not come up in an identical way in every community, but attending to factors beyond motivation will be helpful in most.

**Since the sharing economy is by no means immune to the "build it and they will come" problem, some reasons for failure may not be all that interesting.** Perhaps a new exchange arrangement had no competitive edge over existing systems that were already available for potential users. For instance, in cities where Craigslist is very popular, there may be little to be gained from a niche marketplace for a particular type of good. Even when designed with the best of intentions, a system that is created with little understanding of whether anyone actually has a need for what it has to offer is always unlikely to succeed. While there may not be much of interest in documenting yet another failure of this type, I would argue that it is more common that there are useful insights to be gained from how some initiatives are born and die within relatively short time spans and how others never attract many enough participants or a large enough number of transactions to register as a success (especially if those initiating the exchange arrangement where hoping to grow a business out of it).

**There is room for a critical reflection on what we expect of interpersonal relationships in the context of peer-to-peer exchange.** While early sharing economy narratives positioned strengthened social ties and exciting interactions with strangers as central features of peer-to-peer exchange, it should be clear by now that some caution is warranted. More or less unexamined expectations of the kinds of interpersonal interactions and relational outcomes that peer-to-peer exchange should bring about can trap us into considering our efforts a failure when they might in fact be meeting participants' needs quite well—only the participants may not need or want what the designers expected! Many attempts at peer-to-peer technologies have been evaluated based on their ability to foster deep, meaningful, and/or long-lasting connections between users. Yet, key to future design might rather be aiming seemingly low by seeking interventions that require little of those involved and are careful to respect a social distance where exchange partners wish to maintain it.

**Looking beyond economic value and attempts at scaling up, we can learn from the social and economic alternatives that are already being developed.** While criteria for success often remain implicit, they tend to relate to scale, levels of engagement, and longevity. To consider alternatives, we can think of cooperatives as one example: unlikely to desire unrestricted growth, they may choose different paths, including resistance to growth, purposeful growth, and operating with goals tied to a pragmatic dedication to the widely-scoped benefit to members and principles like solidarity, education, and democratic governance (Lampinen et al., 2018). Much like these member-owned arrangements, peer-to-peer exchange initiatives may struggle to capture and sustain research attention, in part because they do not comply with the ideal of scalability. Yet, not everything needs to go mainstream and succeed as a business—initiatives can be beneficial to those involved without ever attracting broader attention or finding a way to turn a profit. While the narratives around Silicon Valley unicorns provide us with one vision of what success looks like, we should be careful not to take that as the only way in which exchange arrangements can matter. Amidst growing concerns about the societal implications of mainstream platforms, alternative arrangements can teach us about designing for livable, equitable futures.

**Longevity and a steady pace of activity are further characteristics that tend to flourish as unarticulated criteria for success.** It is easy to get stuck on the idea that for an initiative to count as successful, it should last for a long time and attract sustained participation. Sometimes, though, an intentionally short-lived pop-up is exactly what is neede—fit-for-purpose and lean in its requirements of time and other resources. Moreover, a seemingly short-lived effort can also be enough to serve as an experiment and teach us valuable lessons that can be brought forward to future efforts. None of this is to deny that some important dynamics are observable only over longer periods of time and that there is value in arrangements that members can rely on over time. This is especially true when it comes to initiatives that challenge another characteristic that is often taken for granted: a reliance on high engagement. When it comes to peer-to-peer exchange, especially the co-use of underutilized physical goods, it seems typical that individuals participate only every now and then when a need arises. For such arrangements to work, they need to be so easy to maintain that it is not a problem that people tap into them only now and then. Alternatively, rather than setting up a structure that is intended to be available all the time, organizing around events can be effective. This is what flea markets and car boot sales excel at: they take place within a limited time slot but may then be repeated, for instance seasonally, if that seems well-motivated. From an HCI point of view, these types of approaches challenge a single-minded focus on exchange platforms, prioritizing, instead, events. This means that any technological support that is relevant here might need to look drastically different from platforms that are set up to serve as continuously operating multi-sided marketplaces.

**Finally, exchange arrangements may fail even when they look successful.** We should be critical of arrangements that do relatively well in terms of attracting a group of active participants but, simultaneously, fail miserably in terms of their values of inclusion—deepening social divides rather than bridging them (Schor, 2020). While we should be careful not to cast efforts as failures too quickly, we should be equally cautious not to celebrate as successes initiatives that attract active participation over extended periods of time, if at once they are not capable of living up to the values they set out to foster.

# Epilogue

When we design new exchange platforms, we inherently adopt some assumptions about a social system—or create a new one. Markets are made, produced, and sustained by those involved in their functioning (Lampinen and Brown, 2017). Markets are human-created systems and, as such, it is up to us to fix them if they are broken, intervene when they are failing, and start new ones where they can be useful (Roth, 2015). Casting markets as human artifacts turns them into objects of design and critical scrutiny, and as such, more explicitly objects of study for HCI scholars. Beyond the exchange arrangements this book has focused on, there are many more we can work to improve —and endless others we could create.

Since markets are often instantiated in a technological form, the HCI community can take an active role in designing markets and intervening critically where they do not work fairly or effectively. This is not easy, and it will not do away with the fundamental interpersonal issues that peer-to-peer exchange entails. Yet, we are not powerless to intervene in existing systems or to create future alternatives. Just as we need to understand social relationships and interpersonal communication to design successful, or provocative, social media systems, insight into markets can help us create effective yet socially acceptable mechanisms for allocating resources and matching people. Studying peer-to-peer exchange and designing systems that help people to navigate the interpersonal challenges it entails is one important avenue for developing livable—and even desirable—futures.

This book is, first and foremost, an invitation to attend to the interpersonal issues that make peer-to-peer exchange so fraught with failure and yet so appealing. There are ripe opportunities for creating exchange arrangements that strike the contextually right balance between the convenience of assured transactions and the cherished social qualities that can only come into being through interpersonal effort. But the interpersonal is never disconnected from the (infra)structural. Over the past decade, platforms have become an increasingly dominant infrastructural and economic model for describing and understanding the social web. While profit-driven platforms have captured most of the attention in conversations about the sharing economy, they are not all that there is. We need to consider and create alternatives to how exchange arrangements function—and who owns and governs them. This is crucial not only as part of our broader efforts of designing technologies that are effective and enjoyable to engage with, but also because these systems play increasing roles in how people come together, consume, and get by in their daily lives.

# References

Acquier, A., Daudigeos, T., and Pinkse, J. (2017). Promises and paradoxes of the sharing economy: An organizing framework. *Technological Forecasting and Social Change*, 125, 1–10. DOI: 10.1016/j.techfore.2017.07.006. 2, 3, 5

Adler, J. (1985). Youth on the road: Reflections on the history of tramping. *Annals of Tourism Research*, 12(3), 335–354. DOI: 10.1016/0160-7383(85)90003-9. 21

Alkhatib, A., Bernstein, M. S., and Levi, M. (2017). Examining crowd work and gig work through the historical lens of piecework. *Proceedings of the 2017 CHI Conference on Human Factors in Computing Systems*, 4599–4616. DOI: 10.1145/3025453.3025974. 24

Altman, I. (1975). *The Environment and Social Behavior: Privacy, Personal Space, Territory, Crowding*. Brooks/Cole Pub. Co. 7, 47, 48

Altman, I. (1977). Privacy regulation: Culturally universal or culturally specific? *Journal of Social Issues*, 33(3), 66–84. DOI: 10.1111/j.1540-4560.1977.tb01883.x. 47

Altman, I. and Gauvain, M. (1981). A cross-cultural and dialectic analysis of homes. In *Spatial Representation Behavior Across the Life Span. Theory and Application*. Academic Press. 47, 48, 49

Antin, J. (2009). Motivated by information: Information about online collective action as an incentive for participation. *Proceedings of the ACM 2009 International Conference on Supporting Group Work*, 371–372. DOI: 10.1145/1531674.1531729. 65

Balestra, M., Arazy, O., Cheshire, C., and Nov, O. (2016). Motivational determinants of participation trajectories in Wikipedia. *ICWSM*, 535–538. 65

Balestra, M., Cheshire, C., Arazy, O., and Nov, O. (2017). Investigating the motivational paths of peer production newcomers. *Proceedings of the 2017 Chi Conference on Human Factors in Computing Systems*, 6381–6385. DOI: 10.1145/3025453.3026057. 8, 65

Bannon, L. J. and Ehn, P. (2012). Design matters in participatory design. *Routledge Handbook of Participatory Design*, 37–63. 25

Barta, K. and Neff, G. (2016). Technologies for sharing: Lessons from quantified self about the political economy of platforms. *Information, Communication and Society*, 19(4), 518–531. DOI: 10.1080/1369118X.2015.1118520. 5

90   **REFERENCES**

Baumber, A., Scerri, M., and Schweinsberg, S. (2019). A social licence for the sharing economy. *Technological Forecasting and Social Change*, 146, 12–23. DOI: 10.1016/j.techfore.2019.05.009.75

Baym, N. K. (1995). The emergence of community in computer-mediated communication. APA PsycNet®. 24

Baym, N. K. (2000). *Tune In, Log On: Soaps, Fandom, And Online Community* (Vol. 3). Sage. 24

Baym, N. K. (2018). *Playing To the Crowd: Musicians, Audiences, and the Intimate Work of Connection* (Vol. 14). NYU Press. DOI: 10.18574/nyu/9781479896165.001.0001. 24

Belk, R. (2010). Sharing. *Journal of Consumer Research*, 36(5), 715–734. DOI: 10.1086/612649. 3, 20

Belk, R. (2014). You are what you can access: Sharing and collaborative consumption online. *Journal of Business Research*, 67(8), 1595–1600. DOI: 10.1016/j.jbusres.2013.10.001. 3

Bellotti, V., Ambard, A., Turner, D., Gossmann, C., Demkova, K., and Carroll, J. M. (2015). A muddle of models of motivation for using peer-to-peer economy systems. *Proceedings of the 33rd Annual ACM Conference on Human Factors in Computing Systems*, 1085–1094. http://dl.acm.org/citation.cfm?id=2702272. DOI: 10.1145/2702123.2702272. 8, 25, 63, 65

Bellotti, V., Carroll, J. M., and Han, K. (2013). Random acts of kindness: The intelligent and context-aware future of reciprocal altruism and community collaboration. *Collaboration Technologies and Systems (CTS)*, 2013 International Conference On, 1–12. http://ieeexplore.ieee.org/xpls/abs_all.jsp?arnumber=6567197. DOI: 10.1109/CTS.2013.6567197. 4

Bellotti, V. M., Cambridge, S., Hoy, K., Shih, P. C., Handalian, L. R., Han, K., and Carroll, J. M. (2014). Towards community-centered support for peer-to-peer service exchange: Rethinking the timebanking metaphor. *Proceedings of the SIGCHI Conference on Human Factors in Computing Systems*, 2975–2984. http://dl.acm.org/citation.cfm?id=2557061. DOI: 10.1145/2556288.2557061. 25

Berns, K., Rossitto, C., and Tholander, J. (2021a). *"This is not a free supermarket": Reconsidering Queuing at Food-sharing Events*. DOI: 10.1145/3461564.3461582. 25

Berns, K., Rossitto, C., and Tholander, J. (2021b). Queuing for waste: Sociotechnical interactions within a food sharing community. *Proceedings of the 2021 CHI Conference on Human Factors in Computing Systems*, 1–15. DOI: 10.1145/3411764.3445059. 25

Bialski, P. (2012a). Becoming intimately mobile. Peter Lang Frankfurt, Germany. http://www.peterlang.com/download/datasheet/62848/datasheet_263070.pdf. DOI: 10.3726/978-3-653-01584-3. 21, 43, 45, 49, 50, 54, 57, 68, 72, 73

Bialski, P. (2012b). Technologies of hospitality: How planned encounters develop between strangers. *Hospitality and Society*, 1(3), 245–260. DOI: 10.1386/hosp.1.3.245_1. 49, 72

Blau, P. M. (1986). *Exchange and Power in Ssocial Life*. Transaction Books.19, 34

Bødker, S. and Klokmose, C. N. (2012). Dynamics in artifact ecologies. *Proceedings of the 7th Nordic Conference on Human-Computer Interaction: Making Sense Through Design*, 448–457. DOI: 10.1145/2399016.2399085. 4

Bødker, S., Korsgaard, H., and Saad-Sulonen, J. (2016). "A farmer, a place and at least 20 members": The development of artifact ecologies in volunteer-based communities. *Proceedings of the 19th ACM Conference on Computer-Supported Cooperative Work and Social Computing*, 1142–1156. DOI: 10.1145/2818048.2820029. 4

Bødker, S., Lyle, P., and Saad-Sulonen, J. (2017). Untangling the mess of technological artifacts: investigating community artifact ecologies: Full paper. *Proceedings of the 8th International Conference on Communities and Technologies*, 246–255. DOI: 10.1145/3083671.3083675. 4

Boehner, K. and DiSalvo, C. (2016). Data, design and civics: An exploratory study of civic tech. *Proceedings of the 2016 CHI Conference on Human Factors in Computing Systems*, 2970–2981. DOI: 10.1145/2858036.2858326. 25

Brotherton, B. (1999). Towards a definitive view of the nature of hospitality and hospitality management. *International Journal of Contemporary Hospitality Management*. DOI: 10.1108/09596119910263568. 20

Buchberger, S. (2012). Hospitality, secrecy and gossip in Morocco: Hosting CouchSurfers against great odds. *Hospitality and Society*, 1(3), 299–315. DOI: 10.1386/hosp.1.3.299_1. 49, 72 73

Carroll, J. M. (2014). *The Neighborhood in the Internet: Design Research Projects in Community Informatics*. Routledge. DOI: 10.4324/9780203093573. 25

Carroll, J. M. (2013). Co-production scenarios for mobile time banking. *International Symposium on End User Development*, 137–152. DOI: 10.1007/978-3-642-38706-7_11. 75, 79

Carroll, J. M. and Rosson, M. B. (2013). Wild at home: The neighborhood as a living laboratory for HCI. *ACM Transactions on Computer-Human Interaction (TOCHI)*, 20(3), 1–28. DOI: 10.1145/2491500.2491504. 25

Cheshire, C. (2007). Selective incentives and generalized information exchange. *Social Psychology Quarterly*, 70(1), 82–100. DOI: 10.1177/019027250707000109. 19

Cheshire, C. (2011). Online trust, trustworthiness, or assurance? *Daedalus*, 140(4), 49–58. DOI: 10.1162/DAED_a_00114. 8, 65

Cheshire, C. and Antin, J. (2008). The social psychological effects of feedback on the production of Internet information pools. *Journal of Computer-Mediated Communication*, 13(3), 705–727. DOI: 10.1111/j.1083-6101.2008.00416.x. 19

Cheshire, C. and Antin, J. (2009). *Order, Coordination and Uncertainty. Etrust: Forming Relationships in the Online World*. Russell Sage Foundation Publications, New York, 266–291. 19

Cheshire, C., Gerbasi, A., and Cook, K. S. (2010). Trust and transitions in modes of exchange. *Social Psychology Quarterly*, 73(2), 176–195. DOI: 10.1177/0190272509359615. 34, 56

Cook, K. S. and Cheshire, C. (2013). Social exchange, power, and inequality in networks. *The Handbook of Rational Choice Social Research*, 185–219. 56

Cook, K. S. and Emerson, R. M. (1978). Power, equity and commitment in exchange networks. *American Sociological Review*, 721–739. DOI: 10.2307/2094546. 19

Cook, K. S. and Emerson, R. M. (1984). Exchange networks and the analysis of complex organizations. *Research in the Sociology of Organizations*, 3(4), 1–30. 19, 34

Cook, K. S., Snijders, C., Buskens, V., and Cheshire, C. (2009). *Etrust: Forming Relationships in the Online World*. Russell Sage Foundation. 20, 65, 80

Cook, K. S., Yamagishi, T., Cheshire, C., Cooper, R., Matsuda, M., and Mashima, R. (2005). Trust building via risk taking: A cross-societal experiment. *Social Psychology Quarterly*, 68(2), 121–142. DOI: 10.1177/019027250506800202. 20, 65

Cooke, B. and Kothari, U. (2001). *Participation: The New Tyranny?* Zed books. 63

Costanza-Chock, S. (2020). *Design Justice: Community-Led Practices to Build the Worlds We Need*. The MIT Press. https://library.oapen.org/handle/20.500.12657/43542. DOI: 10.7551/mitpress/12255.001.0001. 78, 81, 84

de La Bellacasa, M. P. (2017). *Matters of Care: Speculative Ethics in More than Human Worlds* (Vol. 41). University of Minnesota Press. 5, 77

Dillahunt, T. R., Wang, X., Wheeler, E., Cheng, H. F., Hecht, B., and Zhu, H. (2017). The sharing economy in computing: A systematic literature review. *Proceedings of the ACM on Human-Computer Interaction*, 1(CSCW), 1–26. DOI: 10.1145/3134673. 18

Dubal, V. B. (2020). The time politics of home-based digital piecework. *Center for Ethics Journal: Perspectives on Ethics, Symposium Issue "The Future of Work in the Age of Automation and AI*, 50. DOI: 10.2139/ssrn.3649270. 24

Edelman, B. G. and Luca, M. (2014). Digital discrimination: The case of airbnb. com. *Harvard Business School NOM Unit Working Paper*, 14–054. http://papers.ssrn.com/sol3/papers.cfm?abstract_id=2377353. DOI: 10.2139/ssrn.2377353. 69

Ekeh, P. (1974). Social exchange theory. *The Two Traditions*. 19, 35

Emerson, R. M. (1972a). Exchange theory, part I: A psychological basis for social exchange. *Sociological Theories in Progress*, 2, 38–57. 20, 46, 78

Emerson, R. M. (1972b). Exchange theory, part II: Exchange relations and networks. *Sociological Theories in Progress*, 2, 58–87. 20, 46, 78

Fedosov, A., Lampinen, A., Odom, W., and Huang, E. M. (2021). A dozen stickers on a mailbox: physical encounters and digital interactions in a local sharing community. *Proceedings of the ACM on Human-Computer Interaction, 4(CSCW3)*, 1–23. DOI: 10.1145/3432939. 4, 25

Fedosov, A., Odom, W., Langheinrich, M., and Wakkary, R. (2018). Roaming objects: Encoding digital histories of use into shared objects and tools. *Proceedings of the 2018 Designing Interactive Systems Conference*, 1141–1153. DOI: 10.1145/3196709.3196722. 25

Ferreira, P., Helms, K., Brown, B., and Lampinen, A. (2019). From nomadic work to nomadic leisure practice: A study of long-term bike touring. *Proceedings of the ACM on Human-Computer Interaction, 3(CSCW)*, 111:1-111:20. DOI: 10.1145/3359213. 22

Friedman, B. and Hendry, D. G. (2019). *Value Sensitive Design: Shaping Technology with Moral Imagination*. MIT Press. DOI: 10.7551/mitpress/7585.001.0001. 84

Ganglbauer, E., Fitzpatrick, G., Subasi, Ö., and Güldenpfennig, F. (2014). Think globally, act locally: A case study of a free food sharing community and social networking. *Proceedings of the 17th ACM Conference on Computer Supported Cooperative Work and Social Computing*, 911–921. DOI: 10.1145/2531602.2531664. 25, 63

Gillespie, T. (2010). The politics of "platforms." *New Media and Society*, 12(3), 347–364. DOI: 10.1177/1461444809342738. 23

Glöss, M., McGregor, M., and Brown, B. (2016). Designing for labour: Uber and the on-demand mobile workforce. *Proceedings of the 2016 CHI Conference on Human Factors in Computing Systems*, 1632–1643. DOI: 10.1145/2858036.2858476. 23

Gouldner, A. W. (1960). The norm of reciprocity: A preliminary statement. *American Sociological Review*, 161–178. DOI: 10.2307/2092623. 33

Gurran, N. and Phibbs, P. (2017). When tourists move in: how should urban planners respond to airbnb? *Journal of the American Planning Association*, 83(1), 80–92. DOI: 10.1080/01944363.2016.1249011. 74

Gurran, N., Zhang, Y., and Shrestha, P. (2020). "Pop-up" tourism or "invasion"? Airbnb in coastal Australia. *Annals of Tourism Research*, 81, 102845. DOI: 10.1016/j.annals.2019.102845. 8, 63, 74

Gurstein, M. (2007). *What Is Community Informatics (And Why Does It Matter)?* (Vol. 2). Polimetrica sas. DOI: 10.15353/joci.v3i1.2381. 25

Harper, F. M., Frankowski, D., Drenner, S., Ren, Y., Kiesler, S., Terveen, L., Kraut, R., and Riedl, J. (2007). Talk amongst yourselves: Inviting users to participate in online conversations. *Proceedings of the 12th International Conference on Intelligent User Interfaces*, 62–71. http://dl.acm.org/citation.cfm?id=1216313. DOI: 10.1145/1216295.1216313. 65

Hosio, S., Goncalves, J., Lehdonvirta, V., Ferreira, D., and Kostakos, V. (2014). Situated crowdsourcing using a market model. *Proceedings of the 27th Annual ACM Symposium on User Interface Software and Technology*, 55–64. http://dl.acm.org/citation.cfm?id=2647362. DOI: 10.1145/2642918.2647362. 22

Ikkala, T. and Lampinen, A. (2014). Defining the price of hospitality: Networked hospitality exchange via Airbnb. *Proceedings of the Companion Publication of the 17th Acm Conference on Computer Supported Cooperative Work and Social Computing*, 173–176. DOI: 10.1145/2556420.2556506. 10, 12, 34, 44, 48

Ikkala, T. and Lampinen, A. (2015). Monetizing network hospitality: Hospitality and sociability in the context of AirBnB. *Proceedings of the 18th ACM Conference on Computer Supported Cooperative Work and Social Computing*, 1033–1044. DOI: 10.1145/2675133.2675274. 10, 12, 34, 42, 44, 45, 48, 55, 57, 65, 75

Ilten, C. (2015). "Use your skills to solve this challenge!": The platform affordances and politics of digital microvolunteering. *Social Media+ Society*, 1(2). DOI: 10.1177/2056305115604175. 4, 23

Jenkins, H. (2009). *Confronting the Challenges of Participatory Culture: Media Education for the 21st Century*. The MIT Press. DOI: 10.7551/mitpress/8435.001.0001. 63

John, N. A. (2017). *The Age of Sharing*. John Wiley and Sons. 5, 17, 25

Kelty, C. M. (2013). From participation to power. *The Participatory Cultures Handbook*, 22–31. 63

Klein, M., Zhao, J., Ni, J., Johnson, I., Hill, B. M., and Zhu, H. (2017). Quality standards, service orientation, and power in airbnb and couchsurfing. *Proceedings of the ACM on Human-Computer Interaction, 1(CSCW)*, 1–21. DOI: 10.1145/3134693. 61

Kollock, P. and Braziel, E. R. (2006). How not to build an online market: The sociology of market microstructure. *Advances in Group Processes*, 23, 283–306. DOI: 10.1016/S0882-6145(06)23011-X. 22

Kraut, R. E. and Resnick, P. (2012). *Building Successful Online Communities: Evidence-Based Social Design*. MIT Press. DOI: 10.7551/mitpress/8472.001.0001. 8, 65

Lambton-Howard, D., Olivier, P., Vlachokyriakos, V., Celina, H., and Kharrufa, A. (2020). Un-platformed design: a model for appropriating social media technologies for coordinated participation. *Proceedings of the 2020 CHI Conference on Human Factors in Computing Systems*, 1–13. DOI: 10.1145/3313831.3376179. 25

Lampinen, A. (2015). Deceptively simple: Unpacking the notion of "sharing." *Social Media+ Society*, 1(1). DOI: 10.1177/2056305115578135. 5

Lampinen, A. (2016). Hosting together via Couchsurfing: Privacy management in the context of network hospitality. *International Journal of Communication*, 10, 20. 9, 12, 45, 48, 50

Lampinen, A. and Brown, B. (2017). Market design for HCI: Successes and failures of peer-to-peer exchange platforms. *Proceedings of the 2017 CHI Conference on Human Factors in Computing Systems*, 4331–4343. DOI: 10.1145/3025453.3025515. 5, 8, 21, 23, 62, 65, 71, 87

Lampinen, A. and Cheshire, C. (2016). Hosting via Airbnb: Motivations and financial assurances in monetized network hospitality. *Proceedings of the 2016 CHI Conference on Human Factors in Computing Systems*, 1669–1680. DOI: 10.1145/2858036.2858092. 10, 12, 34, 42, 44, 45, 48, 55, 56, 57, 65

Lampinen, A., Huotari, K. J. E., and Cheshire, C. (2015). Challenges to participation in the sharing economy: the case of local online peer-to-peer exchange in a single parents' network. *Interaction Design and Architecture (s)*. Available at http://www.mifav.uniroma2.it/inevent/events/idea2010/doc/24_1.pdf. 9, 11, 25, 70

Lampinen, A., Lehtinen, V., Cheshire, C., and Suhonen, E. (2013). Indebtedness and reciprocity in local online exchange. *Proceedings of the 2013 Conference on Computer Supported Cooperative Work*, 661–672. http://dl.acm.org/citation.cfm?id=2441850. DOI: 10.1145/2441776.2441850. 9, 11, 34, 36, 70

Lampinen, A. M. (2014). Account sharing in the context of networked hospitality exchange. *Proceedings of the 17th ACM Conference on Computer Supported Cooperative Work and Social Computing*, 499–504. http://dl.acm.org/citation.cfm?id=2531665. DOI: 10.1145/2531602.2531665. 9, 34, 44, 48, 50, 54, 73

Lampinen, A., McGregor, M., Comber, R., and Brown, B. (2018). Member-owned alternatives: exploring participatory forms of organising with cooperatives. *Proceedings of the ACM on Human-Computer Interaction, 2(CSCW)*, 1–19. DOI: 10.1145/3274369. 24, 65, 85

Lampinen, A., McMillan, D., Brown, B., Faraj, Z., Cambazoglu, D. N., and Virtala, C. (2017). Friendly but not friends: designing for spaces between friendship and unfamiliarity.

*Proceedings of the 8th International Conference on Communities and Technologies*, 169–172. DOI: 10.1145/3083671.3083677. 61, 81

Lane, J. (2018). *The Digital Street*. Oxford University Press. DOI: 10.1093/oso/9780199381265.001.0001. 69

Lauterbach, D., Truong, H., Shah, T., and Adamic, L. (2009). Surfing a web of trust: reputation and reciprocity on CouchSurfing.com. *Computational Science and Engineering, 2009. CSE '09. International Conference On*, 4, 346–353. DOI: 10.1109/CSE.2009.345. 65

Lawler, E. J. and Yoon, J. (1993). Power and the emergence of commitment behavior in negotiated exchange. *American Sociological Review*, 465–481. DOI: 10.2307/2096071. 19, 34

Lehdonvirta, V. (2018). Flexibility in the gig economy: Managing time on three online piecework platforms. *New Technology, Work and Employment*, 33(1), 13–29. DOI: 10.1111/ntwe.12102. 24

Lehdonvirta, V. and Castronova, E. (2014). Virtual Economies: Design and Analysis. MIT Press.https://mitpress.mit.edu/books/virtual-economies.   DOI:   10.7551/mitpress/9525.001.0001. 22, 23

Lepper, M. R. and Greene, D. (2015). *The Hidden Costs of Reward: New Perspectives on the Psychology of Human Motivation*. Psychology Press. DOI: 10.4324/9781315666983. 65

Light, A., and Miskelly, C. (2015). Sharing economy vs sharing cultures? Designing for social, economic and environmental good. *Interaction Design and Architecture(s)*, 24(Spring), 49–62. 25

Light, A., and Miskelly, C. (2019). Platforms, scales and networks: Meshing a local sustainable sharing economy. *Computer Supported Cooperative Work (CSCW)*, 28(3–4), 591–626. DOI: 10.1007/s10606-019-09352-1. 15, 80

Ling, K., Beenen, G., Ludford, P., Wang, X., Chang, K., Li, X., Cosley, D., Frankowski, D., Terveen, L., and Rashid, A. M. (2005). Using social psychology to motivate contributions to online communities. *Journal of Computer-Mediated Communication*, 10(4), 00–00. DOI: 10.1111/j.1083-6101.2005.tb00273.x. 65

Lingel, J. (2020). *An Internet for the People: The Politics and Promise of Craigslist*. Princeton University Press. DOI: 10.1515/9780691199887. 22, 69, 83

Lynch, P., Di Domenico, M., and Sweeney, M. (2007). *Resident Hosts and Mobile Strangers: Temporary Exchanges Within the Topography of the Commercial Home*. http://oro.open.ac.uk/11578/. 53

Mair, J., Robinson, J., and Hockerts, K. (2006). *Social Entrepreneurship* (1st ed.). Palgrave Macmillan, London. DOI: 10.1057/9780230625655_1. 25

Malinowski, B. (1922/2014). *Argonauts of the Western Pacific*. Routledge. DOI: 10.4324/9781315772158. 18

Malmborg, L., Light, A., Fitzpatrick, G., Bellotti, V., and Brereton, M. (2015). Designing for sharing in local communities. *CHI EA '15: Proceedings of the 33rd Annual ACM Conference Extended Abstracts on Human Factors in Computing Systems*, 2357–2360. DOI: 10.1145/2702613.2702645. 63

Markus, M. L. (1987). Toward a "critical mass" theory of interactive media universal access, interdependence and diffusion. *Communication Research*, 14(5), 491–511. DOI: 10.1177/009365087014005003. 8, 65

Mauss, M. (1925/2002). *The Gift: The Form and Reason for Exchange in Archaic Societies*. Routledge. 18

McCarthy, J. and Wright, P. (2015). *Taking [a] Part: The Politics and Aesthetics of Participation in Experience-Centered Design*. MIT Press. DOI: 10.7551/mitpress/8675.001.0001. 63

Molm, L. D. (1988). The structure and use of power: A comparison of reward and punishment power. *Social Psychology Quarterly*, 108–122. DOI: 10.2307/2786834. 19, 35

Molm, L. D. (1997). Risk and power use: Constraints on the use of coercion in exchange. *American Sociological Review*, 113–133. DOI: 10.2307/2657455. 19, 35

Molm, L. D., Schaefer, D. R., and Collett, J. L. (2009). Fragile and resilient trust: Risk and uncertainty in negotiated and reciprocal exchange. *Sociological Theory*, 27(1), 1–32. DOI: 10.1111/j.1467-9558.2009.00336.x. 56

Molz, J. G. (2012). CouchSurfing and network hospitality: "It's not just about the furniture". *Hospitality and Society*, 1(3), 215–225. DOI: 10.1386/hosp.1.3.215_2. 21, 43, 45

Molz, J. G. (2014). Toward a network hospitality. *First Monday*, 19(3). DOI: 10.5210/fm.v19i3.4824. 12, 21, 54, 61, 65, 68, 73, 75, 79

Morrison, A. J. and O'Gorman, K. D. (2006). Hospitality studies: Liberating the power of the mind. *CAUTHE 2006: To the City and Beyond*, 453. 21

Mosconi, G., Korn, M., Reuter, C., Tolmie, P., Teli, M., and Pipek, V. (2017). From facebook to the neighbourhood: Infrastructuring of hybrid community engagement. *Computer Supported Cooperative Work (CSCW)*, 26(4), 959–1003. DOI: 10.1007/s10606-017-9291-z. 24, 25

Moser, C., Resnick, P., and Schoenebeck, S. (2017). Community commerce: Facilitating trust in mom-to-mom sale groups on Facebook. *Proceedings of the 2017 CHI Conference on Human Factors in Computing Systems*, 4344–4357. DOI: 10.1145/3025453.3025550. 22, 56

Mullainathan, S. and Shafir, E. (2013). *Scarcity: Why Having Too Little Means So Much*. Macmillan. 71, 83

Muller, M. J. (2007). *Participatory Design: The Third Space in HCI*. CRC Press. DOI: 10.1201/9781410615862.ch54. 25

Nembhard, J. G. (2014). *Collective Courage: A History Of African American Cooperative Economic Thought And Practice*. Penn State Press.. DOI: 10.5325/j.ctv14gpc5r. xiv

Nieuwland, S. and Van Melik, R. (2020). Regulating Airbnb: How cities deal with perceived negative externalities of short-term rentals. *Current Issues in Tourism*, 23(7), 811–825. DOI: 10.1080/13683500.2018.1504899. 74

Nippert-Eng, C. E. (2010). *Islands of Privacy*. The University of Chicago Press. DOI: 10.7208/chicago/9780226584546.001.0001. 49

Orsi, J. (2014). *Practicing Law in the Sharing Economy: Helping People Build Cooperatives, Social Enterprise, and Local Sustainable Economies*. American Bar Association. 24

Osterloh, M. and Frey, B. S. (2000). Motivation, knowledge transfer, and organizational forms. *Organization Science*, 11(5), 538–550. DOI: 10.1287/orsc.11.5.538.15204. 65

Palgan, Y. V., Zvolska, L., and Mont, O. (2017). Sustainability framings of accommodation sharing. *Environmental Innovation and Societal Transitions*, 23, 70–83. DOI: 10.1016/j.eist.2016.12.002. 22

Palmer, A. (2014). *The Art of Asking: How I Learned to Stop Worrying and Let People Help*. Grand Central Publishing. 33

Parigi, P. and State, B. (2014). Disenchanting the world: The impact of technology on relationships. *International Conference on Social Informatics*, 166–182. http://link.springer.com/chapter/10.1007/978-3-319-13734-6_12. DOI: 10.1007/978-3-319-13734-6_12. 62

Petronio, S. S. (2002). *Boundaries of Privacy: Dialectics of Disclosure*. State University of New York Press. 7, 49

Pilemalm, S. (2018). Participatory design in emerging civic engagement initiatives in the new public sector: applying pd concepts in resource-Scarce Organizations. *ACM Transactions Computor-Human Interactions*, 25(1), 5:1–5:26. DOI: 10.1145/3152420. 25

Preece, J. and Shneiderman, B. (2009). The reader-to-leader framework: Motivating technology-mediated social participation. *AIS Transactions on Human-Computer Interaction*, 1(1), 13–32. DOI: 10.17705/1thci.00005. 65

Raval, N. and Dourish, P. (2016). Standing out from the crowd: emotional labor, body labor, and temporal labor in ridesharing. *Proceedings of the 19th ACM Conference on Comput-*

*er-Supported Cooperative Work and Social Computing*, 97–107. http://dl.acm.org/citation.cfm?id=2820026. DOI: 10.1145/2818048.2820026. 23

Resnick, P., Kuwabara, K., Zeckhauser, R., and Friedman, E. (2000). Reputation systems. *Communications of the ACM*, 43(12), 45–48. DOI: 10.1145/355112.355122. 22

Resnick, P. and Zeckhauser, R. (2002). Trust among strangers in internet transactions: Empirical analysis of ebay's reputation system. *The Economics of the Internet and E-Commerce*, 11(2), 23–25. DOI: 10.1016/S0278-0984(02)11030-3. 22

Rheingold, H. (1993). *The Virtual Community: Homesteading on the Electronic Frontier*. MIT Press. 24

Rosen, D., Lafontaine, P. R., and Hendrickson, B. (2011). CouchSurfing: Belonging and trust in a globally cooperative online social network. *New Media and Society*, 13(6), 981–998. DOI: 10.1177/1461444810390341. 65

Roth, A. E. (2008). What have we learned from market design?*. *The Economic Journal*, 118(527), 285–310. DOI: 10.1111/j.1468-0297.2007.02121.x. 78

Roth, A. E. (2015). *Who Gets What—and Why: The New Economics of Matchmaking and Market Design*. Houghton Mifflin Harcourt. 22, 23, 78, 87

Scholz, T. (2017). *Uberworked and Underpaid: How Workers are Disrupting the Digital Economy*. John Wiley and Sons. 24

Scholz, T. and Schneider, N. (2017). *Ours to Hack and to Own: The Rise of Platform Cooperativism, A New Vision for the Future of Work and a Fairer Internet*. OR Books. DOI: 10.2307/j.ctv62hfq7. 24

Schor, J. (2016). Debating the Sharing Economy. *Journal of Self-Governance and Management Economics*, 4(3), 7–22. DOI: 10.22381/JSME4320161. 3

Schor, J. (2020). *After the Gig: How the Sharing Economy Got Hijacked and How to Win It Back*. University of California Press. DOI: 10.1525/9780520974227. 77

Schor, J. B. and Fitzmaurice, C. J. (2015). Collaborating and connecting: The emergence of the sharing economy. In *Handbook of Research on Sustainable Consumption*. Edward Elgar Publishing. DOI: 10.4337/9781783471270.00039. 4

Selwyn, T. (2013). An anthropology of hospitality. *In Search of Hospitality* (pp. 36–55). Routledge. 20

Seyfang, G. (2003). Growing cohesive communities one favour at a time: Social exclusion, active citizenship and time banks. *International Journal of Urban and Regional Research*, 27(3), 699–706. DOI: 10.1111/1468-2427.00475. 4

Seyfang, G. and Smith, K. (2002). The time of our lives: Using time banking for neighbourhood renewal and community capacity building. http://www.citeulike.org/group/14819/article/9699937. 25

Shih, P. C., Bellotti, V., Han, K., and Carroll, J. M. (2015). Unequal time for unequal value: Implications of differing motivations for participation in timebanking. *Proceedings of the 33rd Annual ACM Conference on Human Factors in Computing Systems*, 1075–1084. http://dl.acm.org/citation.cfm?id=2702560. DOI: 10.1145/2702123.2702560. 63

Simmel, G. (1903/1950). The metropolis and mental life. In K. H. Wolff (Ed.), *The Sociology of Georg Simmel* (pp. 409–427). Simon and Schuster. 21, 57, 68

Suhonen, E., Lampinen, A., Cheshire, C., and Antin, J. (2010). Everyday favors: A case study of a local online gift exchange system. *Proceedings of the 16th ACM International Conference on Supporting Group Work*, 11–20. http://dl.acm.org/citation.cfm?id=1880074. DOI: 10.1145/1880071.1880074. 9, 11, 25, 34, 36, 61, 71

Sundararajan, A. (2016). *The Sharing Economy: The End of Employment and the Rise of Crowd-Based Capitalism*. MIT Press. 69, 83

Tan, J.-E. (2010). The leap of faith from online to offline: An exploratory study of couchsurfing. Org. In A. Acquisti, S. Smith, and A.-R. Sadeghi (Eds.), *Trust and Trustworthy Computing* (Vol. 6101, pp. 367–380). Springer Berlin/Heidelberg. http://www.springerlink.com/content/h0p7483550603331/abstract/. DOI: 10.1007/978-3-642-13869-0_27. 65

Tsing, A. L. (2015). *The Mushroom at the End of the World: On the Possibility of Life in Capitalist Ruins.* Princeton University Press. DOI: 10.2307/j.ctvc77bcc. 18, 42

Turner, F. (2005). Where the counterculture met the new economy: The well and the origins of virtual community. *Technology and Culture*, 46(3), 485–512. DOI: 10.1353/tech.2005.0154. 24, 25

Vines, J., Clarke, R., Wright, P., McCarthy, J., and Olivier, P. (2013). Configuring participation: On how we involve people in design. *Proceedings of the SIGCHI Conference on Human Factors in Computing Systems*, 429–438. DOI: 10.1145/2470654.2470716. 63, 72

Vlachokyriakos, V., Crivellaro, C., Le Dantec, C. A., Gordon, E., Wright, P., and Olivier, P. (2016). Digital civics: Citizen empowerment with and through technology. *Proceedings of the 2016 CHI Conference Extended Abstracts on Human Factors in Computing Systems*, 1096–1099. DOI: 10.1145/2851581.2886436. 25

Willer, R., Flynn, F. J., and Zak, S. (2012). Structure, identity, and solidarity: A comparative field study of generalized and direct exchange. *Administrative Science Quarterly*, 57(1), 119–155. DOI: 10.1177/0001839212448626. 34, 36

Yamagishi, T. and Cook, K. S. (1993). Generalized exchange and social dilemmas. *Social Psychology Quarterly*, 235–248. DOI: 10.2307/2786661. 19, 35

Young, I. M. (1997). Asymmetrical reciprocity: On moral respect, wonder, and enlarged thought. *CONS™LATIONS-OXFORD-*, 3, 340–363. DOI: 10.1515/9780691216355-004. 47

Zelizer, V. (2005). *The Purchase of Intimacy*. Princeton University Press. 47, 61

Zuev, D. (2012). CouchSurfing as a spatial practice: Accessing and producing xenotopos. *Hospitality and Society*, 1(3), 227–244. DOI: 10.1386/hosp.1.3.227_1. 49, 54

# Author Biography

**Airi Lampinen** is Associate Professor in Human–Computer Interaction at the Computer and Systems Sciences Department at Stockholm University and a Docent in Social Psychology at the University of Helsinki. She is a founding faculty member of the Stockholm Technology and Interaction Research group and part of Digital Futures Faculty. Her research is focused on interpersonal challenges at the intersections of economic encounters, exchange platforms, and algorithmic systems.

Alongside her pioneering research on peer-to-peer exchange and the sharing economy, Lampinen was instrumental in initiating and running the COST Action From Sharing to Caring: Examining Socio-Technical Aspects of the Collaborative Economy where she co-led the working group on collaborative economy practices and communities. Lampinen holds a Ph.D. in Social Psychology from the University of Helsinki. In addition to her social scientific training, she holds a BSc (Eng.) from Aalto University's interdisciplinary Information Networks degree program.

Printed in the United States
by Baker & Taylor Publisher Services